the Princess journal

A 30 Day Journey of Learning to Live Like a Daughter of The King

Dr. Jill A. Jones

The Princess Journal
by Dr. Jill A. Jones

© 2010 All rights reserveds

All rights reserved. No portion of this book may be reproduced by any means, electronic or mechanical, including photocopying, recording, or by any information storage retrieval system, without permission of the copyright's owner, except for the inclusion of brief quotations for a review.

ISBN-13: 978-0-98193-576-8

Cover & Interior Design:

Megan Johnson
Johnson2Design
Johnson2Design.com

A Division of Liberty University Press
Lynchburg, VA

Dedication

This devotional is dedicated to my husband and sons. Ray, you see the real me; the girl who wants to love God and others and often falls on her face. Thank you for being my biggest fan and always encouraging me to reach for the stars. I still cannot believe you gave up your dream job so I could teach at a Christian university. I often feel God's love through your actions.

Raymond and Niko, thank you for not being embarrassed of a mom who raises her hands in church and falls on her knees in the middle of the kitchen, living room…wherever she is when she is overwhelmed by God's presence. Thank you for being patient with me when I may 'push' God's love too much or too fast. I love being your mom!

Table of Contents

Introduction *1*

Part I: How to Become a Princess

Week 1

Day 1: My Story and Yours *5*
Day 2: Trust *12*
Day 3: Trust and Memory *17*
Day 4: Love *22*
Day 5: An Ambassador for Love *28*

Week 2

Day 6: Being Loving *35*
Day 7: Becoming a Reflective Practitioner *41*
Day 8: A Prayer Warrior *51*
Day 9: The Example of Biblical Prayer Warriors *61*
Day 10: God's Grading System *66*

Week 3

Day 11: Preparing to suffering. *69*
Day 12: Love and Suffering. *75*
Day 13: A Forgiver. *81*
Day 14: One of God's Great Forgivers-David. *85*
Day 15: Forgiveness and God's Unusual Request. *92*

Part II: Dressing Like a Princess

Week 4

A Princess Has a Lovely Mouth

Day 16: Wearing a Mouthguard. *99*
Day 17: Using God's Mouthwash. *104*
Day 18: Washing Your Mouth with Fear and Sorrow?. . *108*
Day 19: Washing Your Mouth with Confession, Submission, and Blood?. *113*
Day 20: Family, Friends, and Fellowship? Can These Three Items Work Together?. *118*

Week 5

The Art of Make-Up & Accessories

Day 21: Applying the perfect brightening serum. *125*
Day 22: Choosing the Right Lip Stick. *130*

Day 23: Adorable Ears. *137*
Day 24: Blood Earrings?. *142*
Day 25: Wearing God-Ordained Princess Sunglasses. . .*146*

Week 6

Feet & Hands

Day 26: Always Pick Your Shoes Carefully-Stilleto Heels. *153*

Day 27: Always Pick Your Shoes Carefully-In-Line Skates. *160*

Day 28: Always Pick Your Shoes Carefully-Spiritual Slippers. *168*

Day 29: Beautiful Busy Hands. *174*

Day 30: Beautiful Up-Lifted Hands. *180*

The Royalty Oath. *186*

About the Author

Jill A. Jones is currently an Associate Professor of Graduate Education at Liberty University in Lynchburg, Virginia. She received her educational doctorate in Reading and Adult Education from Northern Illinois University and is the author of several research articles.

Dr. Jones is a member of Thomas Road Baptist church where she is active in her Sunday school class and serves as a mentor mom. Jill and Ray have been married for twenty years and have two teenage boys, Raymond and Niko.

Jill currently travels the nation presenting at educational and women conferences. Please contact Dr. Jones at, drjillajones@yahoo.com, if you are interested in having her speak at an event and/or organize a conference in your area.

Introduction

Greetings, sisters!

I am thrilled that you are interesting in pursuing your royal heritage. This devotional has been written to act as a supplement to your daily Bible reading and prayer time. I like to think of it as your "princess vitamin;" it doesn't replace your breakfast, it just gives you an added boost.

Each week is broken up into five lessons which should take you about 30 minutes to complete. You can choose to start on Monday and work through Friday, or break it up according to your needs. I have friends who have busy Tuesdays and Wednesdays so they would probably decide to add this devotional work to the other days.

Unless otherwise noted, the NIV Bible translation has been used throughout this study.

May God richly bless your work efforts and draw you near to Him!

Loving You through Him,

Jill

Part I:

How To Become a Princess

Week 1

Day 1: My Story & Yours

Pale blue eyes peeked out between the wood slits into the empty living room. The young girl knew that looks could be deceiving and her worst enemy could be lurking in the shadows just outside her line of vision. "How long will I have to stay hidden in the base of our entertainment center?" was the question that continued to plague the 6-year-old's mind. Jill had only been hidden for a few minutes and her small feet were already beginning to tingle. "I should have taken off my shoes," she whispered to herself. As her young mind began to think of ways to contort her body, she realized that the space was too small for movement and she was just going to have to get used to the discomfort. With a small sigh she closed her eyes and prayed that her parents would return soon.

"Oh Jill, guess what I found!" shouted a voice from upstairs.

Jill's heart began to beat rapidly as she realized in her hurry to find a hiding spot she had left Butterball all alone in her room. Maybe her older sister Luanne hadn't found him. Maybe she was just pretending like the other times she had tricked her ... but what if she had?

Butterball, a small, well-loved, stuffed dog, was Jill's best friend. It was Butterball who played with her in her secret hiding spots. It was Butterball who listened to her and never hurt her. The little girl closed her eyes and pictured Butterball's crescent-shaped eyes and his worn, tan fur.

"I know you are hiding, Jill, but this time I am not going to have to waste my time finding you because you are going to come out and save your little friend."

The voice of her older sister was on the stairs now, and Jill knew she must remain very still. She caught a glimpse of her sister turning on the lights, but the slits in the wood were not big enough to allow her to follow her around the room.

"You know what, Jill, I think Butterball needs a haircut," Luanne stated as she plopped down on the couch. The old plaid couch was in line with Jill's view so she watched in horror as her 11-year-old sister proceeded to cut some of Butterball's fur.

"I am going to be a great hairdresser when I grow up," Luanne said and then looked around the room. She began to snip away at the hair around Butterball's ears.

"Okay!" Jill screamed as she opened up the sliding wood door and scooted out from her hiding spot, "You win, just don't hurt Butterball."

Luanne's cat-like green eyes burned into Jill's and a smile crept slowly across her face. With a quick flick of her wrist she tossed Butterball high onto one of the storage cabinets and glared at her younger sister.

"You know, Jill, that has got to be your best hiding spot yet. I never would have dreamed that you could have fit in the tiny space under the TV. I probably would have never found you if it hadn't been for Butterball."

While Luanne talked, Jill's eyes quickly scanned the room. The only way out would require her to get past her older sister, and she had learned that Luanne could run at lightning speed. Jill quickly decided that reasoning with her older sister was her only option.

"Luanne, why do you hate me so much?" Jill asked in a tone barely above a whisper.

Luanne, expecting her little sister to run, was shocked into momentary silence. Surely, her perfect little sister knew why she was a thorn in her side, everyone in the family knew. Just thinking about what Jill had done brought Luanne's hands into balled fists and fire to her eyes.

"Listen, brat, stalling techniques will not work."

Luanne's harsh words made Jill nervous but she still knew that as long as her big sister kept talking there might be a chance her parents would return before the torture began.

"I really want to know, why don't you like ..."

"LIKE you? You cannot be serious, Jill. I hate you. I hate that you were ever born. I wish you had been the one to die!" Luanne hissed at her pig-tailed, blue eyed, freckled face, adorable, and oh-so-perfect baby sister. "Now, what game will we play today? Maybe a little game of bloody Mary."

Those very words, "bloody mary," made Jill's own blood stand still. This was one of the worst "games" Luanne liked to play; Luanne knew it scared Jill and gave her terrible nightmares.

Jill shook her head back and forth, causing her right pigtail to become entangled in the hinge of the entertainment door and ripping a few strands of hair from her head. The pain, coupled with the memory of the last time they "played" bloody Mary, brought tears to her eyes.

Luanne watched as several tears began to fall from her baby sister's face. She couldn't believe Jill was trying to use tears to influence her. Didn't Jill realize how many times she had cried because of her; those memories came back in a flood and prompted Luanne to grab one of Jill's pigtails and drag her to the bathroom door. With a quick shove, both Luanne and Jill were inside the dark bathroom.

"Okay, brat, you know how this works. You look into the mirror and say, 'bloody Mary' three times and then the ghost of the dead girl will appear."

"Please, Luanne, please ..." Jill pleaded while trying to keep her eyes averted from the mirror she knew was right in front of her.

Luanne's grip was strong on Jill's face and her size alone kept Jill in front of the vanity facing the mirror.

"Say the words, Jill, and let's meet our ghost friend."

"Girls, girls, where are you?" asked their mother from upstairs.

"Say a word of this to Mom and next time will be worse," growled Luanne while shoving Jill out into the bright lights of the living room.

"Mom, we are downstairs playing a game," replied Luanne in her most angel-like voice. "Did you and Dad enjoy your time alone?"

"Yeah," their mother Sandy replied while walking down the stairs.

"You know your father, he likes to get back home and ... ." Sandy's words came to a halt when she saw the tear-stained face of Jill. "Not again," she thought. "Why can't my girls just get along?"

"Why has your sister been crying, Luanne?" her mother asked.

"You know Jill, she is so emotional and her dumb stuffed dog is stuck on the storage shelf," replied Luanne while grabbing Jill's arm tightly.

A sense of relief flooded over Sandy. She knew that if her husband had to deal with any more crying and fighting between the kids that he would not take her out anymore, and she really needed some time away from the kids.

"Oh, well, that is easily fixed," Sandy stated cheerfully while looking at Jill's downcast face. Within minutes she had placed the well-loved animal into Jill's arms and saw her daughter run upstairs, most probably to her bedroom closet. For a moment it occurred to her that Jill spent an awfully large amount of time alone in her dark closet.

"Sandy!" shouted her husband from upstairs, and with those words Sandy forgot about the whole event.

This one vignette allows you to grasp the tone of my childhood: a sister who hated me, a mother who needed some time away, and a father who was too busy to notice her. Doesn't my story have the makings of a Disney classic? Little girl unjustly treated + faithful friends + saving hero = happily every after. Although I do become a princess in the end, the characters in my story are not your typical Disney-folk. In fact, the reason I am writing these chapters is to urge my sisters in Christ to join me in my royal status. Dear, sweet sister, you do not have to live in the cottage while I dine in the castle. I am writing to share my invitation to the palace. The purpose of this Bible study is to show you how to become a princess and then learn to live like one.

No matter how beautiful or troubled your childhood was, nothing compares with the life you begin once you realize *and embrace* the notion that you are royalty. Before we move forward on that journey, I am going to ask you to look back and vividly remember your past.

Jeremiah 1:5 states, "Before I formed you in the womb I knew you, before you were born I set you apart; I appointed you as a prophet to the nations" (NIV).

That verse applies to each of us. Please make that verse personal by filling in the blanks. I completed a few of mine as an example.

"I appointed you as a <u>teacher</u> to <u>children and adults.</u>"
　　　　　　　　　　<u>mother</u> to <u>my boys.</u>"
　　　　　　　　　　　<u>wife</u> to <u>Ray.</u>"

"I appointed you as a _____ to _____."

"I appointed you as a _____ to _____."

"I appointed you as a _____ to _____."

Week 1 · Day 1

"I appointed you as a _____ to
_____."

Ladies, God knows us! Jesus tells us, "And even the very hairs of your head are all numbered" (Matthew 10:30, NIV). My point is: God knows your story. He was there, with you, while it unfolded. My question is, "Do you know your story?" It may seem like a silly question; however, memory is a fragile entity. If People magazine were to write a story about you to tell the world how your life was before becoming a princess, what would they write?

Your Homework:

Take some time to write about your life. Write about what has shaped you into the person you are today. Reading and writing are two interwoven processes; they work together to assist the learner in gaining new skills and insights. In fact, writing often cements your thoughts and creates epiphanies by forcing you to reflect on memories that often get "pushed" aside. Before you begin, pray and ask God to direct your thoughts. Ask Him to give you a vivid picture of your past. It was God who allowed me to remember the story you read today; He will do the same for you. Then just begin writing; trust Him to direct your thoughts.

A great writing technique is to simply begin by writing down adjectives, verbs, and nouns that come to mind. For example, I would have written: frightened, Luanne, missing mom, where is dad, bathroom! …

_____
_____
_____
_____
_____

Week 1 · Day 1

Day 2: Trust

In order to become a princess you must marry a prince, right? Not true. Actually, you just need to meet the Prince and believe that He can save you. What would have happened if Cinderella doubted Prince Charming's ability to save and provide for her? What if she began to ask questions like, "How do I know he is really a prince?"; "What if I don't fit in there?"; "What if he finds out I am a mess?" I believe that Cinderella would have decided it was better playing it safe and having a place to live, even though it was miserable, than risking taking a chance and failing. I don't think Disney would have sold as many movies if that scenario had occurred. Instead, Cinderella *trusts* that the prince is who he says he is and believes that *love* will find a way. Those two words are your "magic" words into the world of royalty; you cannot be a princess of God without them.

Trust—Please read the following verse and fill in the blanks.

John 14:1-4 (NIV) "Do not let your hearts be troubled. Trust in _____; trust also in _____. In my Father's house are many rooms; if it were not so, I would have told you. I am going there to _____ a _____ for you. And if I go and prepare a _____ for you, I will come back and take you with me that you also may be where I am. You know the _____ to the place I am going."

Well ladies, what do you think about that statement! All I can say is, "I get the pink room." Seriously, what is Jesus telling us in these verses?

1. His Father (God) has a big mansion (sounds like a palace to me)

the Princess journal

12

2. He is fixing a special room just for YOU

3. He is coming back to get us. Yes, you read right. He is personally going to come back to take us with him. (Good thing, because I am not so good with directions)

I believe there are two critical aspects to Jesus' promises. First, look at how He starts the verse; He tells us not to worry. Girls and worry, hmmm, don't those two items go together like peanut butter and jelly? Not according to Jesus! He says we can be free from a "troubled" heart by doing what? There is crazy power in the spoken word, so please, say the following words right out loud: "I can be free from worry by *trusting* in God and *trusting* in Jesus!" Did you notice that the trust part is sandwiched between not worrying and going to the mansion?

Now let's visit with the wisest man to walk the Earth (except for Jesus), King Solomon.

Proverbs 3:5-6 (NIV) "Trust in the _____ with all your _____ and lean not on your own _____ . In all your ways acknowledge Him, and He will make _____ _____ .

Have you ever felt like a hamster in a wheel? You are running and running and running, and feeling oh so tired, but getting nowhere. That is how life becomes when we trust our own instincts or rely on the world's advice to bring us happiness. Our paths get all twisted and bent.

Take some time to reflect on your current life situation.

1. What are some of the things you spending most of your energy doing? _____ _____ (cleaning/ shopping/studying/driving/laundry/cooking/teaching/working …)

Week 1 · Day 2

2. Generally, what is the expression on your face while you are doing above stated activity(s)?_____

_____
_____
_____

3. Who or what are you relying on for wisdom and understanding? In other words, who/what do you turn to when you are frustrated? Do you pick up the cell phone and call someone? Do you go shopping? Do you make a big bowl of ice cream? Do you hit your knees and ask God for help? (The advice of your parents, friends, teachers, TV, magazines, boyfriend…) _____

_____
_____
_____
_____
_____
_____
_____
_____
_____

4. On a scale from 1-10, with 10 being a perfect score, how is that process working out for you? _____

I can always tell when I am straying from God because my energies are exerted on my job and the business of taking care of my home. I wake up with a visual "to do" list in my head. My eyebrows are all twisted up with worry lines and doubt creases because I am relying on my sheer energy to get all the items on the list completed. At the end of the day I often feel weary and defeated. However, when I wake up and simply begin thanking my Father for everything that comes to mind and then tell Him: "Today is for you Father; show me who you want me to love today; I trust You and give you my day." I have crazy energy and a smile that survives the chaos of my day.

My favorite part of Proverbs 3:5-6 is when we are told that, "... He will make your paths straight." I am terribly directionally challenged. In fact, I once got lost (for an hour and a half) going from my new home to my job. I think my principal really thought I was lying; no one could get that confused behind the wheel. But, God is so good and helped man create something called Global Positioning Systems (GPS). My husband's new motorcycle has one and it actually talks to him and tells him the most direct route to take to his destination, and if he goes the wrong way it quickly recalculates and brings him back on the direct path. I really need one attached to my purse!

So let's pretend for a minute I have one. I get behind the wheel and type in the address of my destination. I am driving along when it tells me to go right. I think, "Oh man, I knew I shouldn't have bought the on-sale one, this thing is broke. If I go right here it will take me way out of my way and I will be late for my meeting." Then, in all my directional wisdom, I keep going straight. Within a few miles I find myself trapped between cars in a heavy construction zone. Now, because I didn't trust my GPS, I get to sit and reflect upon my error for hours. Hmmm, I wonder how often we do that with God. He tells us to *trust* Him and acknowledge Him in all we do, including driving/shopping/talking on the cell phone/listening to music/cleaning ... and He will make our paths straight.

First and foremost, a Princess trusts her Father; she believes what He tells her.

Your Homework:

Today I am going to ask you to complete a visualization exercise. I want you to close your eyes and picture as many tasks as possible from yesterday. Then ask yourself, "Did I enter that information into God's GPS system and follow His directions? Finally, reflect on the outcome(s).

Activity	God's GPS On/Off	Reflections
Telling my son he cannot drop Spanish 2.	Off	I wonder if I had asked God first if He would have given me a different way to explain my response, a method that would not have frustrated my son.

the Princess journal

Day 3: Trust & Memory

About halfway through a semester, when my undergraduate students are beginning to trust me, I often start my class by telling a student I am going to use her for an experiment. (I always choose a student who I am confident will do well in this situation.) I then say something like this:

"Michelle, I am really impressed with your ability to read and understand the textbook for this class. Your notes truly depict deep understanding and your classroom discussion points bring heightened understanding to the entire class. I am, however, truly disappointed with your effort on the last assignment; I expected greater work from you. On a side note, though, you have such beautiful green eyes."

I make sure I say everything with a smile on my face, an even tone of voice, and that I begin and end on a positive note. What do you think the students always remember — the positive statements or the one critical comment? As soon as I have completed my personal speech, I turn and ask the class this same question. I tell the class that the positive statements were all true and I made up the critical one for this experiment. I then turn to the student who participated in the experiment and ask her what she has been thinking. Oftentimes, the student has been so caught up in the one critical statement that she hasn't even heard that I made it up. She then shares with the class that she immediately forgot the positive statements and her mind began to race over the critical one. Even after the student realized that my critical comment was not true, he/she often approaches me after class in order to confirm that there was no aspect of truth in the critical comment.

I do this experiment with my students to get them to understand the burden and great responsibility a teacher holds. Every word teachers use can positively or negatively impact their students; some words can scar students for life, while others can bring motivation to overcome life's obstacles. At the end of this lecture I write this question on the board, "How do you want your students to remember you?" and ask my students to respond in writing before they leave.

Okay, I realize that many of my sisters are never going to be called into the field of education; so what is my point? My point is simply this: What do you remember most about your life? What memories can conjure up the most poignant visual memories? While many of us have some strong positive memories (the day I got married, the first time my infant son smiled at me), I am afraid it is more likely that we remember the bad things that have occurred. You know what, that is great! Really, I think it is wonderful that you can remember the bad times of your lives. No, I have not lost my mind, I am merely saying that remembering the hard times of your life can lead to a greater relationship with your Father. It is like the famous Footprints poem:

One night I had a dream. I was walking along the beach with the Lord, and across the skies flashed scenes of my life. In each scene I noticed two sets of footprints in the sand. One was mine, and one was the Lord's. When the last scene of my life appeared before me, I looked back at the footprints in the sand, and to my surprise I noticed that many times along the path of my life there was only one set of footprints, and I noticed that it was at the lowest and saddest times in my life. I asked the Lord about it: "Lord you said that once I decided to follow you, you would walk with me all the way. But I notice that during the most troublesome times in my life there is only one set of footprints. I don't understand why you left my side when I needed you most." The Lord said: "My precious child, I never left you during your time of trial. Where you see only one set of footprints, I was carrying you."

–Author Unknown

Your Father loves you and will never leave you, so the hard times in our lives are often the times when we can see and feel His presence. It is important to reflect and remember times in your life when you could feel God's presence or understand that without Him you would have been in serious trouble. Those reflections are a key component to remembering God's presence in your life; however, satan does not want you to remember the part God played in your life, he simply wants you to remember the pain and suffering of the instances. Oftentimes it is difficult to feel the presence of God while we are in the midst of a trial. The pain and hurt are so intense that even when we pray we feel like we are talking to ourselves. Our Father is so cool! He knew that we would often feel alone during trials and that we would forget how He had helped us in the past.

Together, let's explore what God's Word says about remembering.

Read Genesis 9:8-17.

WOW! What does God, the Almighty, the Supreme One, our Father ... do to help Him remember His covenant with us? _____

_____

_____

_____

_____

Although I have heard and read this story many times, this time it really hit me. God, our Father, gave Himself a physical reminder of a covenant He made: the rainbow.

*Gen. 9: 14-16 (NIV) "Whenever I bring clouds over the earth and the rainbow appears in the clouds, **I will remember** my covenant between me and you and all living creatures of every kind. Never again will the waters become a flood to destroy all life. Whenever* *the rainbow appears in the clouds,* ***I will see it and remember*** *the everlasting covenant between God and all living creatures of every kind on the earth."*

TWICE God states that the rainbow will be a reminder to Him of His covenant with man. The Hebrew word for remember is "zakar" (pronounced zaw-kår') and it means to have a memorial or to recall to memory. So in essence, God set up the most beautiful memorial.

Why would God need a memorial? Jesus tells us in Matthew 10:30 that even the very hairs of our head are numbered. Our God does NOT have a memory problem because He knows and remembers the details of every one of our lives. So why did He create this visual memorial? I think our Father did what we often do as parents; He provided an example for us to follow. I believe our Father was modeling a behavior that He knew we should replicate, while also providing us with a tangible reminder that we do not have to fear the rain.

As a member of the royal family it is your obligation to organize and store the "rainbows" in your life. Your Father wants you to remember what He has done for you so you can cling to those memories in the midst of a trial.

Your Homework:

Look up the following memorials and write what they are.

Genesis 28:10-22 _____

_____

_____

Esther 9:23-28 _____

_____

Exodus 12:12-14 _____

_____

_____

Exodus 16:31-33 _____

_____

_____

Luke 22:15-19 _____

_____

_____

What memorials do you currently have? (Wedding ring/purity jewelry/scars/ notes in Bible ....) _____

_____

_____

_____

_____

_____

_____

_____

_____

_____

_____

Day 4: Love

Deuteronomy 6:5 (NIV) "Love the Lord your God with all your _____ and with all your _____ and with all your _____."

Do you get the impression that He wants all of you? Can you imagine if the man in your life loved you in that fashion? I can just picture it now. Ray races home from work because he cannot wait to spend time with me. When he gets home he shares all that is on his heart and mind and pours out his soul. We periodically hold hands while cooking dinner together and he eagerly reads my body language and studies my actions to determine how he can best show his love for me. Yeah, like that really that happens in my house every night. (Don't worry girls, we will get to taming the tongue in a future chapter!)

As silly as my scenario may seem, that type of active love is what God wants from us. But how is that possible? Well, the magic word starts and ends with the letter "T". Yes, good old trust. To love Him, we must trust Him.

Read John 6:25-29.

When the crowd asks, "What must we do to do the works God requires?" Jesus answered, "The work of God is this: to _____ in the one he has sent.'" (verses 28-29; NIV)

Paraphrased "princess style," what must we do to make our Daddy happy? Jesus answered by telling the group of girls to demonstrate their love for their Dad by trusting in the Knight He sent to rescue them from death.

Now read John 8:42-51. This passage is crazy powerful!

When the Jews claimed that God was their father, Jesus replied by saying, "If God were your Father, you would _____ me, for I came from God and now am here. I have not come on my own; but He sent me." (verse 42, NIV)

Then Jesus explains the daily battle of good versus evil that exists in our world.

Jesus, the Son of God, clearly tells us that we have a choice. We can choose to belong to God by believing He sent His Son to die for us and allow us eternal salvation from sin. John 8:43b-44a provides the other choice, *"Because you are unable to hear what I say. You belong to your father, _____ , and want to carry out your father's desire."*

Princess paraphrase: Each girl has one important choice to make. She can hear the words of Jesus and trust that He is her white knight-sent to lead her to the King of heaven. Lack of trust, or an outward decision to trust Jesus, immediately places her in the dark knight's family. The choice is up to you.

I would like you to engage in an important exercise—a technique that should help you understand how God made your brain. So, what happens when you read these words:

Black Horse *White Horse*

Your brain should have immediately conjured up a picture of each item. It probably happened so fast you barely remember it. Let's try another one. What happens when you read these words:

Puppy *Pig*

Week 1 · Day 4 23

Again, you should have had a mental picture for each item.

It's unlikely, though, that these letters crossed your mind:

puppy pig

God hard-wired our brains to store and retrieve data through pictures and metaphors. Here is another example: when you hear the word "beautiful," what comes to mind?

Write it here: _____

Some of you may have pictured a flower, sunset, child's face, etc., but all of you had a picture. Throughout this Bible study I am going to ask you to take the time to draw pictures. It doesn't matter if you aren't a talented artist; it only matters that you take the time to associate a picture with the verse because that process helps your brain organize and store information.

Please draw a picture of the two choices depicted in John 8:42-51:

Choice 1	Choice 2

Let me make this choice personal to you. Please write the name of someone you dearly love here: _____. Picture that person's face. Now fill in that person's name in the following story.

You recently moved to a new area and met a new friend. This person laughs at all your jokes, enjoys your hobbies, and has made time to be there for you on several occasions. You find yourself calling her when you hear good news or are frustrated with a day's event. You are terribly excited to have your new friend meet _____ (name you chose above; my husband's name would go here if I were filling it out). You have invited your new friend over to the house and made sure you cooked all her favorite foods. She enters and gives you a great big hug. You turn to introduce her to _____ and she walks right past to go to the bathroom. You think to yourself, "Oh, my, she really must have had too much water." Soon she meets you in the kitchen and begins helping you get the last-minute food preparation completed. You are laughing and working when _____ walks in the room. _____ walks over to your friend and stretches out a hand. _____ greets her with a warm smile and kind eyes. Your new friend, however, turns her back on _____ and continues the previous conversation. Now you are stunned into silence. Did your new friend just ignore _____, a person you would die for? Doesn't she understand that you love _____? You look your friend in the eyes and say, "Why did you ignore _____?" Her confused eyes meet yours and she calmly states, "I don't believe _____ is that important. Give me some time and I may change my mind. But for now you and I can continue being friends, right?"

Well, could you still have a close relationship with a girlfriend who will not recognize your beloved as being important? How about if your beloved had recently saved her life and almost died for her, yet she still refused to recognize his/her importance?

God, your Heavenly Father, sent His beloved Son to save you from hell. He loves you. But you must choose to recognize Jesus as your Savior. Only by doing this action will you truly be a princess in the most high royal family—God's family.

Week 1 · Day 4

I hope you are ready to join the royal family. It is wonderful! All you need is to trust in Jesus (believe that He is the Son of God and that when He died He saved you from hell) and then embark on the journey to getting know and love your Heavenly Father with all your heart, soul, and mind.

I look forward to playing a small part in helping you get to know and love your King and Father. The first part you must do on your own. No one can make you. You must choose to trust in Jesus and that trust will bring you into His royal family, where He will lead and guide you into becoming the Princess He created you to be.

Be careful, my dear sisters, and do not wait. Satan would love nothing more for you to never find out you are royalty. He knows that he hurts your Father every time you believe the lies (you aren't good enough, you aren't a princess, Jesus—who is that?) and do not accept the fact that you are a child of God; you were born to inherit all the riches of heaven; Jesus is preparing a place for YOU.

If you have never said those words, say them now. "Jesus, oh, how I trust You. I believe that You are the Son of God, and that you came to save me. Thank you for loving me enough to die. Thank you for preparing a place in heaven for me. I am yours. Amen."

Welcome to the family, sister. If you had already trusted in Jesus, take a few minutes to thank Him for that salvation.

Your Homework:

Write your salvation story here. How, when, where, why… did you decide to trust and love Jesus? This story is one of your greatest ways to share the love of God. When people ask you why you are happy/different/peaceful, share this story.

Day 5: An Ambassador for Love

I still remember the day Princess Diana was married. I was in junior high school and the librarian was showing the wedding on her television. It really wasn't the wedding itself that caught my attention; it was the fact that the never-smiling, no-emotions, "shh-ing" librarian was actually holding a box of tissues and standing transfixed before the television. Now that I am an adult I realize that grown women still have dreams of being a princess, and that is probably what that librarian was reliving. At the time I just figured she was madly in love with the prince and sad to see him taken.

When Princess Diana died it wasn't her wedding that people remembered, it was her mission of love. During her brief time as a princess she spent countless hours traveling and bringing encouragement to poverty-stricken and war-torn people. Yes, she had beautiful dresses and servants and money (and her share of unhappiness). So why did she spend so much time giving of herself to others? She could have just "shopped away" her misery, or had affairs, or devoted herself to exercising. I personally believe she gave her love to needy people because they gave her something priceless in return, a feeling of contentment and purpose.

So, princess, what is your purpose in life?

I believe our purpose is to be Ambassadors for Love. Women are emotional creatures. (My husband is shouting a big "AMEN".) We tend to live life through our feelings. We cry at movies, feel sad when our friends hurt, become crazy lionesses when our children/family/friends feel pain and/or disappointment … we literally live life out loud for the world to see. I do not believe these emotions were an accident. I believe they were instilled in us to aid us in our quest to love. But don't just believe me, let's ask Jesus.

Before reading our next Scripture, I want you to think about some of the laws you have to follow. List some of them here.

Examples:

Pay your bills

Don't speed

Do your homework

_____

_____

_____

We often follow these laws because if we don't, there will be consequences. (I got my first and only speeding ticket when I was in college and poor, $72.) Go back to your list and write the consequence for not following the law. For example, not doing your homework will often result in bad grades and bad grades equal the loss of privileges (at least in our house).

Turn to and read Matthew 22:34-40.

Verse 35 (NIV) tells us "an expert in the _____" was testing Jesus.

We have all been tested by "experts," i.e. driving experts allowed or stopped us from getting our driver's license. In each instance, the expert already knows what the "correct" response should be. I think Jesus stymied the "expert" with his answer!

What is the question being asked of Jesus? (v. 36) _____
_____?

YIKES, that question makes the defense of my dissertation topic look like kiddy stuff. At first I thought the question referred to the law found in the Ten Commandments, but then I read them. (Jill's abbreviated version:)

1. He is the only God
2. NO idols
3. Don't use God's name in vain
4. Keep the Sabbath
5. Honor your father and mother
6. Don't murder
7. Don't cheat on your spouse
8. Don't steal
9. Don't tell lies about your neighbors
10. Be happy with what you have

If you were standing in front of a large crowd and an expert in the law asked you to pick just one commandment to be the most important, which one would you pick and why?

Write it here:

_____
_____
_____
_____
_____

Okay, if you are like me you are frustrated. My first notion was to pick #1 about only being one God …but then being a mother, I know that #5 is a biggie. Then there is #7 and I am a big fan of that one (yeah, I want to keep my man all to myself). So the question would have seemed impossible even if the expert had only asked Jesus to simply pick one of the Ten Commandments. But it is much more complicated than that!

I went back to the original question and discovered it had a bigger meaning, "Teacher, which is the greatest commandment in the Law?" Isn't it funny how our preconceived notions interpret what we read? I wanted the question to fit nicely into a multiple-choice answer with Jesus having to pick one of the Ten Commandments.

However, the word *law* in the original Greek is "nomos" (nom'-os) and refers to the first five books of the Old Testament (the Pentateuch).

Can you imagine having to pick the most important, or greatest, law from Genesis, Exodus, Leviticus, Numbers and Deuteronomy?!

I have provided two boxes below that I want you to draw in. (remember my reasoning concerning how your brain works—don't worry if you are not an artist).

Your face when asked this question.	Jesus' countenance when asked this question.
Adjectives that describe how you feel ….	Adjectives that describe how he felt …

I believe Jesus looked at the man and answered him in a matter-of-fact way, just like we would have if someone asked us, "What is your father's biggest law(s)?" Without even pausing I would say, "Leave him and his stuff alone, especially when he is working or tired."

Week 1 · Day 5

What would your response be? _____
_____

Our responses tell a lot about our fathers, don't they! Let's check out Jesus' response about our Father in Heaven.

Matthew 22:37-40 "Jesus replied, "Love the Lord your God with all your _____ and with all your _____ and with all your _____ . This is the first and greatest commandment. And the second is like it: _____ your neighbor as yourself. All the Law and the Prophets hang on these two commandments."

So, ladies, what did we learn about our Father? _____
_____
_____
_____
_____

Can you see why I am so excited that He is actually my Dad, my Papa, my Father! He is nothing like my earthly father (whom I really do love). In order to make God happy I am to love Him and love others. I like to make people happy; I am a people pleaser. For years I tried to make my family happy, especially my Dad, and that is why at the age of 12 I was hospitalized for two weeks with a bleeding ulcer. It is impossible to make all people happy all of the time; however, it is NOT impossible to make God happy. He is not asking you to become a doctor, or cut your hair (yikes!), or have 14 kids (double yikes!); He is asking you to love Him and His precious children. He wants YOU, my dear sister, to be An Ambassador for Love!

Your Homework:

Circle the statement that evokes the strongest emotion.

A. Your neighbor ran over your child's brand new bike.

Your neighbor ran over your brand new bike.

B. Your parents forgot your child's birthday.

Your parents forgot to call you on your birthday.

C. The teacher compliments your child's intellect in front of everyone during Open House.

Your boss gives you a compliment in front of everyone.

D. A drunk driver hit and killed your child.

You are diagnosed with breast cancer.

Now look over your responses. Did you react more to the first or second phrase? I am guessing that your greater emotional response was to the first statements. You can hurt me and I will forgive you pretty quick; however, I have been known to temporarily lose my mind when someone I love is hurt.

The problem is God loves everyone. So we hurt Him when we don't approach *every situation* with an attitude of love.

Week 2

Last week you worked on discovering how God can take your past and use it for His glory. You also spent some time learning about the importance of trust and love. God truly does love you and has great plans for your life. This week continues with the love topic and then moves into reflective thinking and prayer. I pray that you feel God's presence in your life throughout the week!

Day 6: Being Loving

Matthew 22:37-40 "And Jesus replied: 'Love the Lord your God with all your heart and with all your soul and with all your mind. This is the first and greatest commandment. And the second is like it: Love your neighbor as yourself. All the Law and the Prophets hang on these two commandments.'"

Loving sounds easy enough, right? Well, it really wasn't for me. I could love God, when He was working to answer my prayers according to my timelines and wanted responses. I could love my husband and boys, but what about my sister, family, and the other people in my past who had hurt me?

Certainly God didn't mean them. And when He was talking about my neighbors, He really didn't mean the people right next door, who get mad at me if any water accidentally hits their car when I am washing mine, did He?! Yes. After years of struggling to understand and implement God's command, I think I have a good visual that explains why He commands us to love.

Start here:

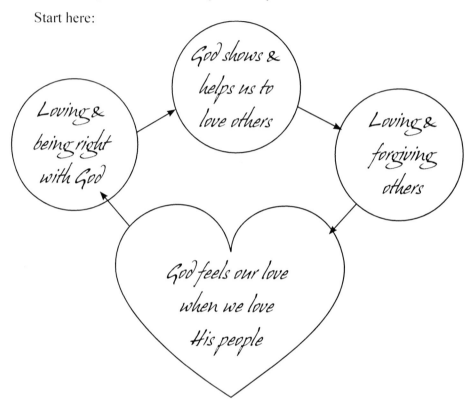

When we love God we spend time trying to get to know Him. We read about Him in the Bible, we talk to Him in prayer, and we spend time with other Christians who talk about Him and His impact in their lives. We strive to know Him. As we draw near to Him we begin to "take on His attributes" and find a greater capacity to love others. The beautiful part of this cycle is the fact that our love for people also demonstrates our love for Him!

Jesus is completely clear in Matthew 5:43-46. Read these verses and then fill in the blanks below.

"But I tell you: Love your _____ and _____ for those who _____ you, that you may be daughters (sons) of your Father in heaven." (44-45, NIV)

This verse spells out the main princess code of ethics. The world will know we are His daughters by our _____!

The converse is also true. Remember how we added consequences to our examples of laws last week? The consequence to not loving God and others is we become distanced from Him. When I first began this process I wouldn't have been too troubled by the consequence; however, after spending time with my Father and feeling the peace that surpasses all human understanding (Phil. 4:7), I never want to be away from Him and feel lost when it begins to happen.

So what does it mean to be An Ambassador for Love? I have written the below vignette to help you better understand this calling.

It is Friday evening and my family is finally all together. Tonight we are blessed with time. The boys don't have basketball practice and Ray doesn't have to work late, coach anything, or attend any meetings. My family is together.

"Let's go to Chili's restaurant for supper," suggests Ray.

"Yay!" shout the boys.

The idea of being waited on while we leisurely discuss the week's events, share our thoughts, and catch up on many topics appealed to me.

"What a wonderful idea," I reply while visions of family time dance in my head.

I quickly call Chili's (it is programmed into my cell phone) and place our name on the waiting list.

Ray drops us off at the front door because the parking lot is full and he will have to park our truck in a distant lot. The boys and I weave our way through the crowd and tell the hostess our name and that we called in already. She smiles and says our table will be ready in a few minutes. The boys and I are already seated when Ray arrives. What a wonderful night.

We quickly decide what we are going to order and then begin talking about our day. More than 10 minutes pass and no one has even stopped by to take our drink order. Having spent many of my college years waiting on tables, I am beginning to get frustrated. Another few minutes pass and Ray asks if I am okay. I tell him I am getting ready to find the manager and give him/her a piece of my mind. Then it occurs to me, "I am a princess and everything I do and say represents my Father." So, I say a quick prayer for help and tell the hostess that our server may not be aware that we are his/her table. The hostess says she will tell the server. Within minutes a young girl appears and takes our drink and dinner order.

"Pheeeww, I think, that was close, I almost lost my witness over a silly thing like that."

But then our appetizer never shows. I, of course, immediately want to use my words to explain to this young girl the importance of timing and other tips on being a good server. This time I don't pray first or remember my title.

"Michelle," I say in my most condescending way. "You do realize that the appetizer should arrive well before the meal otherwise it is not an appetizer!"

The young girl's face turns red and I can feel the eyes of my boys on me.

"I am so sorry, I will fix it right now," the young server stammers as she quickly walks away.

"So," I say in a falsely bright manner, "What were we talking about?"

The boys and Ray continue with the conversation but it is lost to me. I know what I should do and am wrestling with my thoughts and what God is asking of me.

"Michelle," I call out when I see our server walking by. I know if I don't do it now I will talk myself out of it.

The young girl looks at me wearily and approaches.

"I really am working ..." the server begins.

"Michelle, I owe you an apology," I simply state.

The young server stops looking at the table and brings her eyes to meet mine.

"I should never have spoken to you in such an unkind manner. Will you forgive me?"

The young girl smiles and says, "I am sorry, too, I am new and making a lot of mistakes."

We both smile and she leaves. All three of my boys' eyes are on me again. This time I simply say, "Well, I am a princess, you know, and God is represented by everything I say and do. I cannot let this young girl think that it is okay with my Father if I behave rude just because I am hungry. What if she saw us pray for our meal or saw us at church? What kind of witness would I be?"

Ray smiles and we all begin talking again.

That is just one example of what it means to be An Ambassador for Love. Everything we do, ladies, represents our Father so we must be smart and careful about what we say and do. That is why we are in "charm school."

Your Homework:

Let me end this day's lesson with a job for you. Read the following verses from I John 5:14-15 (NASB)

[14] *This is the confidence which we have before Him, that, if we ask anything according to His will, He hears us.* [15] *And if we know that*

He hears us in whatever we ask, we know that we have the requests which we have asked from Him.

These verses mean that all we have to do is ask God to help us love Him more. His Word clearly states that if our request is according to His will, it will be answered. Since our Father commands it, don't you think He will help us learn how! Not a day goes by that I don't ask my Father to teach me, and my family, to love Him more. Guess what? He has!

Pray that prayer right now. Tell your Father that you want His help in learning to love Him. He is not only willing to help you, I have found He is eager to help.

Write your prayer here:

Day 7: Becoming a Reflective Practitioner

*h*ave you ever wanted to get to know someone so badly that sleep no longer mattered? Even when you did sleep your dreams were invaded by the image of that person. You were completely and utterly infatuated and every other aspect of your day was merely a means of getting toward the moment you could see that person. Please allow me to share one of my life stories; I promise there is a point to my storytelling.

It was during my junior year in college that I finally "saw" Ray for the first time. I always knew he was a nice guy; the kind of guy that a girl was comfortable being around and talking to … a good friend. Then my roommate opened my eyes.

"Jill, Ray's at the door and he has the cutest present for you."

"Thanks, Lisa, tell him I will be there in a minute," I replied while quickly finishing what I was reading for class.

I wondered how I was going to tell him that I didn't have much time to spend tonight because I had a test to prepare for and homework in two other classes. "Don't worry about it, Jill," I told myself, "It's Ray, he always understands."

Ray's 6'3" frame filled my dorm room door and his sheepish smile, coupled with the large pumpkin he held, told me that he was not going to be happy with my news. This man had driven over an hour to visit me and he brought me a sweet Halloween present.

My eyes finally crept up from his smile, past his aqua-blue eyes to the space between his eyebrows. Stitches!

"Ray, what happened!"

Week 2 · Day 7

"Oh, these, it's nothing. I just had an untimely accident with the wrong end of my hammer," he nonchalantly replied.

I took the pumpkin, thanked him for the sweet and thoughtful gift and inspected his "owie."

"So, Jill, do you feel up to a walk or shall we drive to the mall and window shop?"

Keeping my eyes on his forehead I replied, *"Let's stay on campus because I don't have much time tonight."*

Ray made sure he masked his disappointment by keeping his voice even. *"No, problem, I have to be at work by 6 a.m. anyways..."*

I did have a nice time that night and Ray dropped me off at my dorm room early so I could study. Our friendship was perfect, no inconveniences. Then my roommate started talking. She went on and on, for almost an hour, about Ray. She talked about how good-looking, sweet, athletic, kind, God-loving, thoughtful, and respectful he is and then asked, "Would you mind if I tried for him since you aren't really boyfriend and girlfriend?" Of course I replied with, "Yeah, no problem, he is a great guy." But that conversation made me think. Why hadn't I seen all those traits before? What if Ray falls for my roommate? Do I really want to share him? That night I did very little studying and a lot of reflecting on the many big and little ways Ray had shown me how much he cares. The way he always opened my car door, the quick trip into the gas station to buy me Tylenol for a headache, his attentive eyes and ears as I talked about past relationships and future dreams, and many more recollections came to mind. How did I miss all of these actions of love? How could I have been so blind and selfish? Then it occurred to me, I had to get to know this man, quick, before my roommate could ensnare him.

It was my conscious decision to get to know Ray that drove my ensuing actions. I began writing him letters, talking on the phone until the wee hours of the night, getting my homework done *before* he would visit, and paying close attention to his body language and facial expressions. Once I realized I was in love with this man, and he was going to marry me, I was like a woman possessed. I asked him every question imaginable. I wanted to know everything. Looking back, I am surprised he didn't lace up his tennis shoes and run! I went from an impassive participant to stalker in zero to 60 seconds. Isn't love grand!

Girlfriends, I tell you that story to give you a clear picture of what God wants from you. I am your roommate and I am telling you that you have a heavenly Father who is the kindest, smartest, selfless, and most thoughtful being you will ever encounter. He has been around your whole life; you may just have missed the greatest parts of His presence. When I look back at my life, I should have died on several occasions. Children left unattended get into trouble. According to my aunt, my sisters and I all had our stomachs pumped more than once because we had digested something lethal. I also did some really stupid stuff as a teenager, such as hitchhiking and spending time with some "interesting" and not-so-moral people. My Father rescued me from more situations than I realized.

I had to reflect on past experiences and my present thinking in order to properly and purposefully alter my actions. I believe that reflection is a key component in becoming a faithful daughter of the King. The below visual depicts the components necessary to becoming a great princess.

Time spent with God through prayer

Self-reflection

Time spent reading God's Word

Reflect—to think, consider, ponder, mull over, contemplate, ruminate, chew on, wonder about, think about, cogitate, deliberate, meditate, to take into account, to weigh up. All these synonyms portray different pictures about the reflection process. The teacher in me wants to ask you to look up each one and draw a picture and/or symbol that depicts how that particular vocabulary word impacts the self-reflection process ... but today's lesson is already long. (Please feel free to do the task if you want to, I believe it will shed light on the process.)

Now let's see what God's Word says about being a reflective practitioner.

Job 37:14 (NIV) "Listen to this, Job; stop and _____ God's wonders."

Remember Job, the man who had everything and then it was all taken away—the man whose friends told him that he was being punished by God even when he declared he had done nothing wrong. In recent years, I had some "abnormal cells" removed from my back. The procedure left a hole the size of a quarter and quite a bit of discomfort. It also made me think about what Job was going through; his whole body was covered in sores. That had to be painful! Why would Job be told to, "stop and consider God's wonders" when he probably had all he could handle just to get through the day?

The Hebrew word for consider is "biyn" (pronounced bene). This word means to "understand." Elihu, a man who had listened to his elders state that Job must have done something wrong and angered God to bring such horrible circumstances, gives Job the same advice I am giving you: stop and reflect upon the wonders of God. Elihu then went on to explain God's great and awesome works. When we reflect on God's greatness, we are reminded that there is nothing that is out of His control and He is still in charge. Those reflections stop the room from spinning and allow us to reign in our self-doubts. Our understanding of the greatness of our Father turns useless worry into productive reflection.

Your Homework:

Your job today is to reflect upon all of the wonders God has performed for you specifically (see chart on next page). As you remember more, add them to your list.

> *Ecc. 7: 13-14 (NIV)* "**Consider** *what God has done: Who can straighten what he has made crooked? When times are good, be happy; but when times are bad* **consider***: God has made the one as well as the other. Therefore, a man cannot discover anything about his future."*

The Hebrew translation of the word "consider" is "ra'ah" (raw-aw') and it means to perceive or inspect. Have you perceived (inspected) your life, what God has done, especially when times are bad?

I believe that King Solomon practiced the art of reflection and as he grew old he felt the hand of God compelling him to share that craft with His children. Ecclesiastes was written when King Solomon had grown old and recovered from his wayward path from God; every time I read Ecclesiastes I can almost feel Solomon's urging to learn from his mistakes and heed his advice.

So, let's try it. Did you ladies notice when Solomon stated we should "consider?" Was it during the good or the bad? _____

Now, I believe he meant both because a true reflective practitioner doesn't have an "on" and "off" switch. Yet, Solomon's emphasis on reflecting during the bad times of life has incredible merit. It was during some of the roughest times in my life that I could consider (perceive and see) the mighty hand of God. Try seeing your Father's presence in your life by simply listing the rough times in your life and then considering His part/presence during those times.

Week 2 · Day 7

I will do a few as an example:

Rough Times	God's Presence
Ray falling off a roof and breaking his pelvis, both wrists, and an elbow.	It was my church family that banded together to show God's love and support. Where did I get the energy from? I had a 2-month-old son and a husband who couldn't walk, feed himself, scratch his nose. Yet, Ray often reminds me of how patient and caring I was. I get impatient if I have to wait in line too long — that patience certainly wasn't on my own accord. Thank you God. I don't think our marriage would have made it without your support.
Raising a teenage son.	Well, this one is harder … maybe because I am in the midst of it. Right now I am relying on my daily conversations with God and my memorized Bible verses to keep me from "physically hurting" my oldest. At times I think that someone else has come to live in his body and has taken away my sweet and kind boy. I guess right now I just have to reflect on God's previous wonders in my life and trust that even if I never figure out where He was during this time, I know that He never left me.

Okay, your turn.

Rough Times	God's Presence

Can you see how considering God's hand in your life, and the lives of others, can help you through times when you may not feel His presence or perceive His reason? I think Elihu, Job's young friend, was the wisest. He reminded Job that even when you cannot see God's hand in your life, you can see it in nature and the mighty works that surround you.

Day 8: A Prayer Warrior

The next few days we will explore communicating with our Heavenly Father. The following depicts my first "baby steps" into talking to my Father. I began by asking His Son for help.

"Jesus."

"Yes, Jill."

"Teach me how to talk to my Heavenly Father."

I am a bit afraid. What if I say something that makes Him angry? Will He punish me? What if I am bothering Him with some small problem, will He get frustrated with me for my lack of faith?

"Help me, Jesus. I don't know how to pray the fancy words like the people on TV."

And Jesus replied...

Matthew 6:5-8 (NIV) [my added interactions are in brackets]

And when you pray [my princess], *do not be like the hypocrites, for they love to pray standing in the synagogues and on the street corners to be seen by men.* [Oh, Jesus, this part is easy for me, I can't image standing in my cul-de-sac shouting prayers so people know I am religious]. *I tell you the truth* [I believe you, Jesus], *they have received their reward in full.* [I don't totally understand what you mean, Lord, but I hope it means that my rewards are still coming.]

But when you pray, go into your room, close the door and pray to your Father, who is unseen. Then your Father [my daddy], *who sees what is done in secret, will reward you.* [I can do this, Lord, but you still haven't told me what to say. What if I make a mistake?]

And when you pray, do not keep babbling like pagans, for they think they will be heard because of their many words. [He knows the inner intentions that drive my outward actions!]

Do not be like them, for your Father knows what you need before you ask him. [Then why does He want me to ask Him?]

Well, ladies, what do you think? Why would our Father want us to vocalize our thoughts; He already knows what we are going to say. (Write your prediction below, by writing it you are forcing your brain to interact with the text and will be able to retain more information.)

_____

_____

_____

_____

We are going to spend several days learning about the power of the spoken word, but for today's purpose we are just going to work toward understanding why God wants us to speak to Him. (Jesus didn't say "if" you pray; He said "when" you pray.)

It is storytime, again.

The smell of fresh, hot, French fries assailed Jill's senses. She was so glad that Ray had suggested they stop and get something to eat; the college cafeteria's fries were always soggy and slightly warm.

"Earth to Jill."

"Oh, sorry Ray, I was just dwelling on the fact that my food will be done any minute and it won't be the cafeteria food."

"You know the cafeteria food is bad when your mouth starts watering in McDonalds," Ray quipped.

The food arrived and Jill immediately began to drench her fries in ketchup. Something about Ray's silence suddenly made her glance his way. Ray's eyes held hers for just a moment and then looked back at his food. The expression on his face made Jill feel a bit uncomfortable. Ray was not his calm self. His brow was all wrinkled up and his eyes held a look of uncertainty.

"Is everything okay, Ray?"

"Uh, yeah, it is just that I have something to tell you, but I think I will wait until later."

Jill's heart began to beat rapidly. Was this bad news? Did he meet someone else? Then she looked up again, this time meeting eyes that were overflowing with love and tenderness. He was going to tell her he loved her, she just knew it, she could see it in his eyes.

"Why wait, Ray, just tell me what you are thinking."

Even though I knew that he was going to tell me he loved me, I desperately wanted to hear the words. Even though Ray knew he loved me, he also knew that once he said those words out loud he was making a commitment. Those spoken words escorted our relationship into a new dimension. In fact, the more we spoke to each other, the better we understood each other, and the closer we grew together.

I am by no means a mind reader, and oftentimes I am clueless as to what my husband is thinking. God is never clueless. He always knows what is on our minds, but I believe He also wants us to declare our commitment to Him by speaking our inward thoughts. It is one thing for me to think, "I need to love my Father" and a whole other dimension for me to say, "Father, I need to love you."

Week 2 · Day 8

Thinking is a conversation with yourself.

Socrates made that statement. I agree. When we are thinking about something, we are really talking to ourselves. Although our Father can read our thoughts, we are not speaking directly to Him. What if Ray never told me what he was thinking and I only learned about him from eavesdropping on his conversations with others? Our relationship would not be very solid. When we merely think our dreams, hopes, and fears we are telling God that eavesdropping is enough. He wants more! He wants a relationship with you, which means you must open your mouth and talk to Him.

Let's pick up where Jesus left off.

Matthew 6:9-13 (NIV) ⁹This, then, is how you should _____. Our Father in heaven, _____ be your name, ¹⁰ Your kingdom come, your _____ be done on earth as it is in heaven. ¹¹ Give us _____ our daily bread. ¹² _____ us our debts, as we also have _____ our debtors. ¹³And lead us not into temptation, but _____ us from the evil one.

There isn't a question you or I could ask that doesn't have an answer in God's Word! Jesus, being God's Son, knows how to communicate with Him. He understands the best way to draw near to Him and create a close relationship. So, ladies, what exactly is Jesus teaching us? Let's break it apart, verse by verse.

Verse 9 "This, then, is how you should _____. Our Father in heaven, _____ be your name,"

Jesus is teaching us HOW to pray and WHO to pray to. Jesus does not tell us to pray to His earthly mother, His disciples, past prophets … Jesus clearly tells us to pray to our Father.

Jesus tells us to call Him, "Father." How very generous of Him.

This reminds me (good readers always make connections to their own lives; as you have them, write them down to share with friends) of a time my oldest son got fighting mad. Ray was coaching his 13 and under travel basketball team and a few of the players started to call him "Dad." My son made it very clear to everyone on the team, "That is your coach, he is MY Father!"

I am so glad that Jesus wants to share with us. Oh, to be selfless like Him.

Verse 10 "Your kingdom come, your _____ be done on earth as it is in heaven."

Jesus is teaching us the importance of recognizing and humbling ourselves to our Father's will. As a new Christian, this concept made me a little nervous. What if God's will was for me to go to Africa and live without air conditioning? But, the more I began to pray, read His Word, and reflect, the closer I came to knowing my Father. He loves me; He really, really, really, loves me. The more I understood that love, (I have such a long way to go!) the more I wanted His will for my life. Let me put it this way, Ray and I love our sons and want them to live a happy life. Either one of us would take our boys' pain and suffering if we could. If we, as imperfect human beings, want the best for our children, think about how great God's will is for our lives.

Verse 11 "Give us _____ our daily bread."

I believe Jesus is teaching us the importance of the "here and now." Check out Matthew 6:34 where Jesus clearly tells us: "Therefore do not worry about tomorrow, for tomorrow will worry about itself. Each day has enough trouble of its own." Do I hear an AMEN, girls?! I used to be the queen of worry. My time spent in prayer, in God's Word, and reflection has helped me reduce my worrying (notice I did not say "eliminate"). What is worrying exactly? In your own words, please define worry and draw a picture or symbol.

Worry

I define worry as "thinking and rethinking and thinking some more about something that I feel is out of my control." My picture would be of me driving, with a cartoon bubble above my head that stated, "Will Niko have a seizure today? Did he get enough sleep last night? Should I stay close to home in case the nurse calls?" My youngest son, Niko, suddenly got epilepsy when he was 8 years old. My mind often turned to worrying when I began to think about his medical condition. Jesus offers the cure to my worrying in verse 11 when he reminds me to ask God for my daily needs. Instead of talking to myself (over and over and over) about Niko, I need to open my mouth and talk to my Father. I have found there is real peace in sharing my concerns with my heavenly Father.

Verse 12 "_____ us our debts, as we also have _____ our debtors."

Forgiveness, what a complex concept and difficult practice! We are going to spend a few days exploring this topic. For today, just realize that Jesus teaches us to ask our Father, daily, for forgiveness and reminds us that we must also give forgiveness. In other words, forgiveness should be a part of our daily prayer life.

Verse 13 "And lead us not into temptation, but _____ us from the evil one."

Jesus teaches us that we NEED our Father to protect us from the evil one. The more I get to know my Father, the scarier this world becomes.

Ephesians 6:12 teaches us, "For our struggle is not against flesh and blood, but against the rulers, against the authorities, against the powers of this dark world and against the spiritual forces of evil in the heavenly realms."

The closer I get to God the more inclined I am to pray for safety and protection from the evil one and his minions. The more I read about the spiritual warfare that surrounds me, the greater my desire to understand how God protects me. I highly recommend all of you girls read Billy Graham's writing on angels ("The Classic Writings of Billy Graham: Angels, How to be Born Again, The Holy Spirit," 2004); his work helped me understand how God uses them.

Below is an excerpt from his book:

In the Old Testament, Daniel vividly describes the bitter conflict between the angelic forces of God and the opposing demons of darkness. Before the angel came to him he had spent three weeks mourning (Daniel 10:3). He ate not bread, meat or wine, nor did he anoint himself. As he stood by the Tigris River, a man appeared clothed in linen. His face looked like lightning and his eyes like flaming torches. His voice sounded like the roar of a crowd.

Daniel alone saw the vision. The men who were with him did not. Yet a great dread came upon them, and they ran away to hide. Left alone with the heavenly visitor, Daniel's strength departed from him, so great was the effect of this personage on him.

Daniel was held in the bonds of a great sleep, yet he heard the voice of an angel. A hand touched him and the angel described an experience he himself had just had. The angel had started to come to Daniel from the moment he began to pray, but en route was waylaid by a demon prince who engaged him in conflict and delayed him. Then Michael came to help this subordinate angel, freeing him to fulfill his mission to Daniel. (pp. 63-64)

Clearly there is a battle going on all around us; I am certain that if our eyes were opened to the "unseen world" that we would be frozen in terror.

Your Homework:

Begin your prayer life today. Start by memorizing Matthew 9-13, or simply writing it out on an index card and keeping it readily available. (You will eventually memorize it.) Then simply follow Jesus' road map for a healthy prayer life by: 1) acknowledging Him as your Father and His holiness, 2) ask for His will to be done in your life, 3) pray about today's needs, 4) ask for forgiveness and for help in forgiving others, and 5) pray for protection. Don't forget to personalize your prayer, your Father wants you to seek Him out and know Him personally.

Try writing your prayer:

_____

_____

_____

_____

Now, the secret to being a prayer warrior is to… REPEAT this process throughout your day. When you find yourself worrying, simply tell your Father about it. When you see a beautiful sunset, whisper a prayer of thanksgiving. When you feel like you are going to do physical harm to a teenager

Week 2 · Day 8

in your house, pray for wisdom and restraint. Whatever is on your mind and heart, tell your Father about it. If you find yourself feeling like your prayers are hitting a ceiling, go back to Jesus' prayer road map and go through the steps; more than once I discovered I had not forgiven myself for something or I was holding forgiveness back from someone. Dear sisters, I am so excited about your journey that I am literally crying. Your prayer life will actually bring you into the loving arms of your Father, the King, and believe me when I say, "Life will never be the same once you have felt His warm embrace!"

Day 9: The Example of Biblical Prayer Warriors

Teaching writing is a difficult endeavor. I have discovered, however, that if I provide an example and details about how the writing will be graded that my students experience greater success. We all need models and clear directions. Today we are going to spend some time with a few of God's prayer warriors. Tomorrow you will spend time exploring God's "grading system" for an effective prayer life. Are you as excited as I am?!

Daniel

Daniel's story begins with him being born into a _____ family (Daniel 1:3). Because he was handsome and smart he was taken captive from Jerusalem to _____ (1:3-4), and given a new "pagan" _____ (1:7).

He was given the title of being a _____ man (1:20) and then decreed to be put to death if he could not recount and interpret the king's dream.

I believe that Daniel knew he needed God and spent time begging God for patience and understanding during Daniel's many trials. My theory is backed by the Bible. When Daniel needed help knowing and interpreting Nebuchadnezzar's dream he, "… returned to his house and explained the matter to his friends Hananiah, Mishael and Azariah. He urged them to plead for mercy from the God of heaven concerning this mystery, so that he and his friends might not be executed with the rest of the wise men of Babylon." (2:17-18)

When God recounted and interpreted king Nebuchadnezzar's dream, Daniel responded by immediately praising God (2:19-23). My favorite portion of this praise is when he says, "He reveals deep and hidden things; he knows what lies in darkness, and the light dwells with him" (2:22).

I believe this early experience created a prayer warrior because Daniel 6:10b clearly depicts his faithful prayer life: "Three times a day he got down on his knees and prayed, giving thanks to his God ...".

Daniel has now served three kings (Nebuchadnezzar, Belshazzar, and Darius). King Darius has seen Daniel's great wisdom. In fact, it was Daniel's interpretation of the writing on the wall that foretold the death of King Belshazzar and the new reign of Darius (Daniel 5:26-34).

Trouble arises for Daniel, though. Daniel 6:3 states: "Now Daniel so distinguishes himself among the administrators and the satraps by his exceptional qualities that the king planned to set him _____ _____ kingdom."

Jealousy, girls, is an ugly sin. One we must avoid and deny entry into our lives. Jealousy causes these men to want Daniel dead. Yet, "They could find no corruption in him, because he was trustworthy and neither corrupt or negligent" (6:4b). They knew Daniel's only area of "weakness," in a pagan culture, "... has something to do with the law of his _____" (6:5b).

They convinced the king to sign an edict that punished anyone who prayed to someone aside from the king.

Daniel's relationship with God enabled him to live a life worthy of being in God's family—even in an extremely pagan culture. Do you think Daniel would have had as much success if he only went to God in prayer during times of trial?

David

God called David, "A man after His _____ _____ (I Samuel 13:14). I honestly believe David was given that amazing compliment because he was a talker and he used that trait to talk to God about everything. Oh, how I want God to see me as a woman seeking after His heart!

We see an example of David's talking skills when he approached Goliath. When David was within speaking distance to the great giant Goliath, he began talking (I Samuel 17:45-47):

David said to the Philistine, "You come against me with sword and spear and javelin, but I come against you in the name of the Lord Almighty, the God of the armies of Israel, whom you have defied. This day the Lord will hand you over to me, and I'll strike you down and cut off your head. Today I will give the carcasses of the Philistine army to the birds of the air and the beasts of the earth, and the whole world will know that there is a God in Israel. All those gathered here will know that it is not by sword or spear that the Lord saves; for the battle is the Lord's, and he will give all of you into our hands."

He talked about God's strength and faithfulness and he attributed the victory to God, before he began fighting.

But his "talking" to men about God pales in comparison to David's constant communication with God.

Please read all of Psalm 3 and underline your favorite verses. This Psalm recounts David's conversation with God after he fled from his son Absalom. My favorite verses are when he writes, "Many are saying of me, 'God will not deliver him.' But you are a shield around me, O Lord; you bestow glory on me and lift up my head" (2-3).

David continually shares his thoughts with God!

Psalm 4:1 depicts David's pleas for help. "_____ me when I call to you, O my righteous God. Give me _____ from my distress; be merciful to me and hear my prayer."

David asks for judgment, "Declare them _____, O God! Let their intrigues be their downfall. _____ them for their many sins, for they have rebelled against you" (Psalm 5:10).

He also spends a great deal of time praising God, "Oh Lord, our Lord, how majestic is your name in all the earth!" (Psalm 8:1).

David wrote about 73 psalms! He loved to talk to God.

I think we gain the best glimpse into David's prayer life, though, by how he responds to the prophet Nathan's message from God. Nathan tells David that his son will die because of his sin with Bathsheba. David's response:

"David _____ _____ _____ for the child. He fasted and went into his house and spent the nights lying on the ground" (2 Samuel 12:16).

Even though David knew God rarely changed his decision, I believe David trusted his relationship with God enough to try talking Him into sparing his son's life!

Your Homework:

Create a prayer routine. Think about your day and write down when you will purposefully enter into conversation with Him. I know a few people who have the "10 at 10" standard. They spend 10 minutes with God at 10 a.m. and 10 p.m. My dear husband talks to God while he is driving. I slide out of bed and hit my knees and immediately begin thanking Him for all I can think of. I also have several other specific times in the day when I purposefully pray.

God is waiting ... will you meet Him?

Day 10: God's Grading System

I was a bit hesitant to use the word "grading" with God because our current system certainly pales in comparison to His ability to judge fairly all the time. However, all of us understand the concept of grading: people striving to meet expectations and receive a corresponding outcome that depicts our efforts. "A" means we have achieved the goals and demonstrated excellence. "B" implies that we have come close to excellence but have fallen just short of that conclusion. "C" generally means we are average and similar to the majority of other students; we didn't demonstrate excellence and we didn't fail the objectives. "D" designates that we barely met the minimal requirements for the stated objective and "F" clearly means we have failed to demonstrate any understanding of the stated goals/objectives.

So, how would God grade our prayer life? His Word is clear about His expectations for us.

Basic Requirements:

1. We must strive to have a Pure Heart _____
   Psalm 66:18-19: "If I have cherished sin in my heart, the Lord would not have _____; but God has surely _____ and heard my voice in prayer."

2. Belief
   Matthew 21:21-22: "Jesus replied, 'I tell you the truth, if you have faith and do not _____, not only can you do what was done to the fig tree, but also you can say to this mountain, 'Go, throw yourself into the sea,' and it will be done. If you _____, you will receive whatever you ask for in prayer."

3. The Name of Christ
   John 14:13-14: "And I will do whatever you ask in _____ _____, so that the Son may bring glory to the Father. You may ask me for anything in _____, and I will do it."

4. God's Will
   I John 5:14-15: "This is the confidence we have in approaching God: that if we ask anything according to _____, He hears us. And if we know that He hears us _____ we ask, we know that we have what we asked of Him."

Educators like to use rubrics to grade. Students tend to like them even more because they give specific information about how the item will be graded. I picture the following prayer rubric. (Again, please keep in mind that grades are man-created and this rubric is my feeble attempt to measure my prayer life.)

Your Homework:

I fully believe that "she who does the most work also does the most learning." Therefore I only completed the first section according to my lens. Take the time to fill the remainder. I pray this work opens your eyes to ways to improve your prayer life. There is CRAZY POWER in prayer.

	A	B	C	D	E
Pure Heart	• Constantly striving to filter this world through daily reading and applying God's Word. • Creates and maintains an accountability system where other Christians remind, encourage, and caution you.	• Strives to filter this world through God's Word. • Creates an accountability system where other Christians remind, encourage, and caution you.	• Reads God's Word. • Has Christian friends.	• Sometimes reads God's Word. • Closest friends are not necessarily Christians, but they are good people.	• Does not read God's Word. • Does not see the need of Proverbs 27:17 ("As iron sharpens iron so one man sharpens another.")
Belief					
The Name of Christ					
God's Will					

Week 3

Day 11: A Princess Will Suffer

Our Father loves us! He really, really does. He has loved us from the minute we were born. In fact, He will never, ever, leave us or let us down; His love is sufficient. But Satan does not want us to believe that truth. Satan wants us to believe that we are all alone and that we are not part of the royal family. I want to share with you a story from the Bible that helped me to understand that God wants me to run to Him for help in *every* situation. He wants me to ask Him to make me "all better" and, most importantly, He wants me to embrace His mercy and behave like a forgiven and healed woman.

II Samuel 13:1-22 (Jill's paraphrased version)

Once upon a time there was a beautiful princess named Tamar. She was the daughter of the great King David and experienced all the wonders of her title. She wore a long beautiful robe and had servants that took care of her. She was so beautiful that her half-brother, Amnon, loved to gaze upon her beauty. Over time Amnon became smitten by Tamar's beauty and could think of nothing else but her. He became so obsessed with Tamar that he began to make himself sick. Amnon's obsessive thoughts brought about a deep depression;

he even began to lose his appetite. Instead of going to his father, the King, for advice, Amnon decided he would worry about the problem himself. Then Amnon's cousin, Jonadab, (he always makes me think of Simba's evil uncle in the movie The Lion King) asked him what was troubling him. Upon learning that Amnon was upset because he could not have Tamar, Jonadab cooked up a sinister plan. He told Amnon to pretend like he was sick and to stay in his room until his father, King David, worried and came to see him. [The fact that Jonadab knew King David would worry allows us to see how much David loved his children!] Then Amnon was instructed to tell his father that he would feel better if Tamar came and took care of him.

Well, Amnon bought into this evil scheme. He just loved the idea of having Tamar alone in his bedroom. The only problem was, Tamar did not come alone. In fact, she brought several people with her. Remember, she was a princess and knew that she must be careful not to do anything that would tarnish her Father's reputation. Tamar entered Amnon's room and baked him fresh bread. The only problem was that when she brought it to him he screamed at all the people to go (I think he said something like "I can't eat with all you people here, you make me feel like I am in a circus — be gone, my sister can take care of me.") So the people left Tamar and Amnon did the unthinkable—he raped her.

Now that the deed was over, Amnon felt disgusted with himself and therefore with Tamar. (I believe he was embarrassed that he was so weak, and discovered that all the years of longing for Tamar were a fantasy and the real thing was nothing like the lies that Satan had been feeding him.) So, he behaved horribly and shoved her out of his room and locked the door behind her. Now sweet Tamar stood in her father's house and had a decision to make. She could go and tell her father what had happened and ask him to help her heal, or she could run and hide. Poor Tamar, I believe she looked at her face in the mirror and saw a ruined woman. She saw a woman that no man could ever want. She saw a woman who had no one who could help her. So, she tore her robe, put ashes on her head, and gave up. Yes, you read it right, she gave up! In fact, the Bible says in verse 20: "So Tamar lived as a desolate woman in Absalom's (her brother's) house."

Okay, sister, if you are anything like me you feel that poor Tamar was innocently led into a horrible situation. So why was she abused? My honest answer is, only our God knows. But the more time I spend in God's Word, the better I begin to understand the possibilities and to trust God's heart.

Jesus, God's son, speaks the truth in love in John 16:33.

*"I have told you all of this so that you may have peace in me. Here on earth you will have many **trials** and **sorrows**. But take heart, because I have overcome the world." (New Living Translation)*

Jesus clearly lets us know that life is not going to be easy. In fact, He delineates that we will have times of testing through trials AND sad sorrows. Life will be hard. I am coming to understand, though, that God will always rescue us in our time of sorrow in one of three ways. Please read the following scriptures and complete the sentences.

1. *He can rescue us **from** the sorrow.*
    A. John 4:46-51: Jesus healed
    B. Matthew 8:23-27: Jesus saved the disciples
    C. Exodus 12:12-13: God rescued the Israelites

Week 3 · Day 11

2. *He can rescue us* **in the midst** *of sorrow.*

   A. Exodus 1:22 & 2:1-3 This mother was in great sorrow because _____ . God rescued her while in her sorrow by saving Moses' life and then later allowing her to _____ (Exodus 2:9) her own son.

   B. Genesis 37:33-36 Jacob is in great sorrow because _____ _____ .

   According to Genesis 44:27-29, Jacob's sorrow lasted a long time. However, God allowed this suffering because (Genesis 45:5-8) _____ _____ . God was working on Jacob's rescue the entire time he sorrowed. God even allowed Jacob to _____ (Genesis 47:10) the _____ and live by Joseph in the _____ land (vs. 11).

3. *He can rescue us* **by removing** *all sorrow.*

   A. In 1Kings 19:3-4 Elijah prays to God to _____ . In verse 14 Elijah pleads his case with God. God's first reply is to have Elijah (1 Kings 19:15-16) anoint _____, _____, and _____ . But God does rescue Elijah from all past, present, and future sorrow by (2 Kings 2:11)
   .

   B. Acts 7:54-60 depicts how God rescued Stephen by allowing him to see "…the glory of God, and he saw Jesus standing in the place of honor at God's right hand….", and then Stephen _____ .

   C. The moist poignant example of God rescuing us from all sorrows occurs in Luke 23: 40-43 when Jesus rescues the criminal on the cross next to Him by saying, "I assure you, today you will _____ ." (verse 43)

I pray that you noticed that in all three rescue methods God's people still endured trials. The nobleman (John 4:46-51) whose child was saved from death still endured the trial of watching his child become ill. Our life will be full of trials. It is how we handle these times that demonstrate our royal status. Do we trust our Father's heart, and offer forgiveness and trust when we don't understand our circumstances? Do we turn to Him for healing and understanding? Keep in mind, sisters, that if we don't turn to our Father, Satan is eagerly waiting to fill our minds with lies. Satan wants us to believe that God does not love us. He wants to buy the lie, "How can such a great and loving God allow you to suffer?" Too many of my dear sisters have believed this lie. Jesus told us we would suffer. Didn't He suffer while He was here among us? Did that suffering stop Him from loving and trusting God? No, it did not, because Jesus has an intimate relationship with the Father. We must strive for that relationship. We must work earnestly to get to know our Father's heart so we can *rest in that love* when we don't understand the world around us.

Don't you wish the Bible showed us Tamar realizing how much her Father loved her? Instead of II Samuel 13:20b stating, "So Tamar remained desolate in her brother Absalom's house," it could have read, "So Tamar prayed to her Heavenly Father for help and understanding. As she prayed, her face shown like an angel as God replaced her torn and tattered clothes with ones He had fashioned for her. Tamar's encounter with God brought healing to her family." Oh, how I pray God keeps me close to Him so I remember His great love for me in all circumstances.

Your Homework:

How has God saved you from sorrow? Write down these specific times and the trials you faced leading up to them.

Has God allowed you to encounter great sorrow and later revealed Himself through it? If so, how? If He hasn't revealed Himself (yet), take this time to reflect and write about the experience. Try to remember Moses' mom and Jacob … God has not forgotten about you … trust His heart!

Day 12: Love and Suffering

The little boy jammed his tear-stained face as deep into the pillow as his breathing would allow. "How can my mommy be so cruel?" he thought to himself; "I didn't mean to run into the street ... I was only trying to get my football." The little boy's eyes dried and were suddenly replaced by an angry scowl. "How can my mommy say she loves me and then spank me and put me in time out!"

A young mother was kneeling and praying from across the room. "Oh Father, please forgive my fear. I cannot seem to shake the vision of my precious son running out in the road. Help him to understand that I love him even when I must discipline him. I don't like having to spank him. It hurts so much. How else can I get him to understand the dangers of running into the road, Father? I told him about how he had an aunt who died because she ran across the street and was hit by a car. Yet, today he still ran in the road. Father, he looked so mad at me. How do I show him I love him ... even when I must allow him to sit in the time-out chair to reflect upon his choices?"

This vignette depicts one scene from my early parenting years. I detested spanking and disciplining my boys. It seemed to go against everything in me—to purposefully cause my sons to feel pain or sadness. I would die for these children and yet I must allow them to feel pain? I cannot imagine how difficult it must be for our Heavenly Father to allow us to endure hardship and pain. He loves us more than I could ever love my boys. Yet, we often react to pain by lashing out at the One who loves us. Can you imagine how I would have felt if my son refused to talk to me or accept my embrace when he was allowed to leave the time-out chair? What if he looked me straight in the eyes and told me, "I don't believe in mommies anymore. Mommies cannot exist because a mommy wouldn't allow her son to feel bad." Ouch! I believe you understand where I am trying to take you. My dear sisters, we must love our Father even when we endure suffering. More importantly, we must trust His plan for our life and His constant presence.

In order to accomplish this task, we must be armed with the knowledge of what our Father feels, says, and believes about us so we are prepared to fight off Satan's lies. A person's actions dictate their true feelings about us. It is one thing to say "I love you" but the actions demonstrate the depth of the love. I know my earthly father loved me; he would often tell me when he thought I was sleeping. However, his actions made me realize he cared more about meeting his physical and emotional needs than mine.

Oh sisters, I cannot wait for us to explore the actions of our Heavenly Father. I have written Psalm 139 into a table format to allow you to picture our Father's actions and how those behaviors impact you. A good reader is always visualizing the printed word and making connections to her past experiences. I want this knowledge, how much God our Father loves us, to stay with you so you can use it to fight off Satan's lies. Working through the scripture by personalizing it will allow your brain to store these truths in a manner that allows you to quickly retrieve it! I have provided two examples for you; please add your own information in those areas also.

Psalm 139	(New Living Translation)	God's Action	My Connection/Thoughts
1	O Lord, you have examined my heart and know everything about me.		
2	You know when I sit down or stand up. You know my every thought when far away.		
3	You chart the path ahead of me and tell me where to stop and rest. Every moment you know where I am.	• He is my personal guide, directing my feet, making sure I get enough rest and that I stop so I don't miss anything • He is my hero, He always knows where I am	Father, I did not realize that you loved me so much to take on the roles of personal guide and protector, those are time-consuming positions! They remind me of when our children were very young. When they were learning to walk we cleared the path, picked them up for a rest, and saved them from electric outlets, sharp corners, stairs... Those years were emotionally and physically draining! I remember feeling like I never rested because I always had to keep an eye on them. The fact that you love me so much to treat me with that kind of tender direction and protection blows my mind; I can't wrap my mind around that kind of love. Help me to understand Your love so I can trust it more.

Psalm 139	(New Living Translation)	God's Action	My Connection/ Thoughts
4	You know what I am going to say even before I say it, Lord.		
5—6	You both precede and follow me. You place your hand of blessing on my head. Such knowledge is too wonderful for me, too great for me to know!		
7	I can never escape from your spirit! I can never get away from your presence!		
8	If I go up to heaven, you are there; if I go down to the place of the dead, you are there.		
9—10	If I ride the wings of the morning, if I dwell by the farthest oceans, even there your hand will guide me, and your strength support me.		

Psalm 139	(New Living Translation)	God's Action	My Connection/ Thoughts
11—12	I could ask the darkness to hide me and the light around me to become night—But even in darkness I cannot hide from you. To you the night shines as bright as day. Darkness and light are both alike to you.		
13-14	You made all the delicate, inner parts of my body and knit me together in my mother's womb. Thank you for making me so wonderfully complex! Your workmanship is marvelous — and how well I know it.		
15	You watched me as I was being formed in utter seclusion, as I was woven together in the dark of the womb.		
16	You saw me before I was born. Every day of my life was recorded in your book. Every moment was laid out before a single day passed.		
17-18	How precious are your thoughts about me, O God! They are innumerable! I can't even count them; they outnumber the grains of sand! And when I wake up in the morning, you are still with me!		

Our Father loves us so much He allowed Jesus to suffer and die (John 3:16); again, I do not understand a love like that and I don't think I am alone in that feeling. End today's time with God by asking Him to help you understand how much He loves you. The more you realize how much He loves you, the more precious you begin to feel, the more you begin to act like the royal princess you are!

Your Homework:

Write your prayer to God. Ask Him to show you how much He loves you.

Day 13: A Forgiver

Joseph was Jacob's favorite son. He loved him so much that he even gave him a special coat of many colors. Jealousy, one of Satan's favorite weapons, caused Joseph's brothers to hate him. In fact, the sin of jealousy spurred these boys to plot Joseph's murder (Gen. 37:18). The brothers did not murder Joseph, but they did sell him into slavery and trick their father into thinking he was dead.

Now fast forward many years. Joseph has been, "… put in charge of the entire land of Egypt" (Gen. 41:41). His brothers are starving in Canaan and have been directed to go to Egypt to purchase grain. These boys must now ask for help from the very brother they sold into slavery. If this scene was taking place in Hollywood, the brothers would pay for their crimes. However, Joseph is a man who walks with God. In fact he says, "I am Joseph, your brother whom you sold into Egypt. But don't be angry with yourselves that you did this to me, for God did it. He sent me here ahead of you to preserve your lives" (Gen. 45:4-5, New Living Translation).

Joseph saw God's hand at work in his life, in the good and bad times. In fact, Joseph continued to pursue a relationship with God.

As a slave—Potiphar, the man who purchased Joseph as his slave, noticed that, "The Lord was with Joseph and blessed him greatly…" (Gen. 39:2).

In jail—"But the Lord was with Joseph there, too….." (Gen. 39:21).

The Pharaoh's worker—"Who can do it better than Joseph? For he is a man who is obviously filled with the spirit of God …" (Gen. 41:38).

To be a true forgiver, a princess must continually spend time in her Father's presence.

How does God want us to forgive?

1. Forgiveness without exceptions.

Forgiveness God's way will not make sense to the world or to you oftentimes!

For example, Saul enjoyed killing God's children. In fact, when Stephen was stoned to death, "Saul was right there, congratulating the killers" (Acts 7, The Message). The Bible goes on the tell us that "... he made havoc of the church, entering every house and dragging off men and women, committing them to prison" (Acts 8:3, NKJV).

This man killed and tortured God's children. Saul was a truly evil man who was, "… eager to destroy the Lord's followers …" (Acts 9:1b). Yet, God states, "Saul is my chosen instrument to take my message to the Gentiles and to kings, as well as to the people of Israel" (Acts 9:15b).

Dear sisters, can you imagine pursuing someone who hurt your family? Picture a serial killer (Saul purposefully killed Christians) attacking your family. Could you forgive that person and then welcome him into your family? My human weakness must confess I do not think I could love someone who murdered and tortured my family. Yet God loved us while we were yet sinners. He loved us so much He allowed His son to die for us. As His daughters we must continue that family tradition.

2. The Holy Spirit imposes us to forgive without waiting for a request for forgiveness.

Acts 7: 55 states that Stephen was full of _____ _____ _____ .

As a result, *as the people were stoning him,* he cried out, "Lord, do not charge them with this sin." (NKJV) In other words, Stephen did not want them blamed for this sin. He forgave them.

Jesus was being led out to be crucified along with two other criminals. In route Jesus said, "Father, _____ these people, because they don't know what they are doing" (Luke 23:34). That kind of forgiveness requires a piece of God within us—the work of the Holy Spirit.

God's Word is completely clear regarding forgiveness. Jesus states in Matthew 6: 14-15, "If you forgive those who sin against you, your heavenly Father will forgive you. But if you refuse to forgive others, your Father will not forgive your sins." Jesus is teaching us the importance of daily forgiving others and also asking forgiveness for our mistakes. This verse does not imply we who are saved will lose that salvation; rather, I believe it allows us to see the chasm that unforgiveness creates in our relationship with God. I once read that unforgiveness, jealousy, and bitterness are sins against the *Holy Spirit* because they hinder His ability to work through us. In other words, those emotions stop me from loving the people who have hurt me and that withheld love puts distance between my Father and me.

Your Homework:

It is important that you pray and ask God to open your eyes to anyone from whom you might be withholding forgiveness. Use the following chart to help you reflect on past hurts and the forgiveness process.

Name	What Happened	Have I Forgiven This person?	How I Know…
My Mom	Pretending to be sick for attention … going to the hospital for a "vacation" from her kids.	Yes	When I pray I feel God's presence. I can feel God's work in my life.

Day 14: One of God's Great Forgivers – David

Teachers often use a model or example to assist their students in understanding or visualizing a new task. For example, if I were going to teach my class how to write an expository, persuasive essay, I would have them watch me go through the thinking, outlining, and writing process. Then I would have them try the thinking and outlining process in pairs while I walked around the room to monitor and assess each student's understanding of this task. I would then gradually release students to begin working on their new writing projects as I detected their heightened awareness of this task.

I believe God has given us some powerful and clear examples of God-inspired forgivers: King David and Hosea. Today we will follow David's example.

King David: Forgiving when the world accepts and expects other actions.

David is faithful to Saul. I Samuel 18:5 states, "Whatever Saul sent him to do, David did it so successfully that Saul gave him a high rank in the army. This pleased all the people, and Saul's officers as well" (NIV).

So how does the king react? Saul becomes *jealous of or happy for* (circle the correct one) David because the people attribute "tens of thousands" of deaths to David and only "thousands" to King Saul (I Samuel 18:7).

In fact, Saul attempts to personally kill David by _____ at him TWICE (I Samuel 18:10-11).

How does David respond to these actions?

1. He works to stay alive by "eluding" the king's efforts to kill him.

2. He continues to give 100% of his efforts while working for the king.

I cannot imagine anyone would have faulted David for planning a takeover of the kingdom. The people loved David and many of them saw King Saul attack him for no apparent reason. Yet, David forgives and trusts God to lead his actions.

Now the politics of the royal life come into play. King Saul attempts to end David's life by:

1. Sending David out to _____ (I Samuel 18:12-13).
2. Using emotional warfare.

"One day Saul said to David, 'Here is Merab, my eldest daughter. I want to give her to you as your wife. Be brave and bold for my sake. Fight God's battles!' But all the time Saul was thinking, 'The Philistines will kill him for me. I won't have to lift a hand against him.' David, embarrassed, answered, 'Do you really mean that? I'm from a family of nobodies! I can't be son-in-law to the king.' The wedding day was set, but as the time neared for Merab and David to be married, Saul reneged and married his daughter off to Adriel the Meholathite" (I Samuel 18:17-19, The Message).

I picture David saying, "Do you really mean that?" and feeling like Saul might really love him after all. I believe we have all experienced this feeling. People tell us something they know we want to hear, but they really don't mean it ... and once we realize the truth we are hurt.

3. Setting unfair _____ (I Samuel 18:25). Saul asks for 100 Philistine foreskins in exchange for marrying his other daughter, Michal. The Philistines were a scary bunch of men. Judges 15:9-11 demonstrates how the people feared these men.

4. Hiring hit men (I Samuel 19:1). In fact, Saul tells his own _____ to kill David.

5. _____ a spear at David while he played the harp for Saul, again (I Samuel 19:9-10)!

6. Hiring _____ men, again (I Samuel 19:14, 20, 21)!

7. Personally going to find and _____ David (I Samuel 19:22).

8. Sending his _____ , again, to find David and bring him to his death (I Samuel 20:30-31).

9. Killing all the _____ in order to scare others into telling Saul where David hides (I Samuel 22:17-18).

10. Searching steadfastly in the _____ for David (I Samuel 23:14).

11. Hiring spies to find out and monitor David's hiding places (I Samuel 23:23).

12. Passionately pursuing David (I Samuel 23:26-29 & 24:2).

Week 3 · Day 14

I believe you are getting the picture. Saul attempted to harm, hurt, injure, mangle, destroy, annihilate … David. Did David commit any crimes? No, in fact he was completely innocent. When David asks Jonathan if he committed a crime or wronged Saul, Jonathan clearly states, "Never!" (I Samuel 20:1-2).

According to the world's standards, David should seek vengeance, kill Saul, and claim the throne. That movie would make money at the box office. However, David is a great forgiver because he does not pursue the world's path.

I Samuel 24:1-7 depicts the scene in which David has the perfect opportunity to kill Saul. In fact, his men counsel David to commit this deed by saying, "This is the day the Lord spoke of when he said to you, 'I will give your enemy into your hands for you to deal with as you wish'" (v. 4).

David does not kill Saul. Not because he was afraid or unable because David truly was a killing machine—so much so that God didn't allow him to build His temple (I Chronicles 28:3).

These are the words David spoke to Saul:

"This day you have seen with your own eyes how the Lord delivered you into my hands in the cave. Some urged me to kill you, but I spared you; I said, 'I will not lift my hand against my master, because he is the Lord's anointed'" (I Samuel 24:10).

David goes on to explain his plan of dealing with the major injustices in his life:

"Now understand and recognize that I am not guilty of wrongdoing or rebellion. I have not wronged you, but you are hunting me down to take my life. May _____ _____ judge between you and me. And may _____ _____ avenge the wrongs you

have done to me, but my hand will not touch you. As the old saying goes, 'From evildoers come evil deeds,' so my hand will not touch you" (1 Samuel 24:11b-13).

Wow, right? If you are like me you might be thinking, "Is this the same man who committed the sin of killing Uriah" (2 Samuel 11:14-27)? Yes, that David is the same David of great forgiveness portrayed above. However, this younger David had to fully rely on God for every aspect of his life; that reliance filled David with the Holy Spirit. Later on David was the King and appeared to forget to rely on God daily. I believe this sad truth is why Jesus stated, "How hard it is for the rich to enter the kingdom of God" (Mark 10:23b)!

Psalm 63 was written by David when he was hiding out in the wilderness from King Saul. In fact, chronologically speaking, this Psalm was written shortly before David had his first opportunity to kill Saul. As you are reading this Psalm please underline all the aspects that show David's dependence on God and put an asterisk by the items that depict the *relationship that ensued.

O God, You are my God;
Early will I seek You;
My soul thirsts for You;
My flesh longs for You
In a dry and thirsty land
Where there is no water.
So I have looked for You in the sanctuary,
To see Your power and Your glory.
Because Your lovingkindness is better than life,
My lips shall praise You.

Thus I will bless You while I live;
I will lift up my hands in Your name.
My soul shall be satisfied as with marrow and fatness,
Any my mouth shall praise You with joyful lips.
When I remember You on my bed,
I meditate on You in the night watches.
Because You have been my help,
Therefore in the shadow of Your wings I will rejoice.
My soul follows close behind You;
Your right hand upholds me.
But those who seek my life, to destroy it,
Shall so into the lower parts of the earth.
They shall fall by the sword;
They shall be a portion for jackals.
But the king shall rejoice in God;
Everyone who swears by Him shall glory;
But the mouth of those who speak lies shall be stopped.

David's dependence resulted in him: seeking, thirsting, longing, looking for, praising, blessing, lifting his hands in honor, having joyful lips, remembering, meditating, following closely, and rejoicing in God! We must implement these same practices when we are in a trial and do not know the way out.

David's relationship with God is seen by: David calling Him "my God," "my Help," and feeling Him protecting him in the shadow of His wings and upholding him from death.

Your Homework:

Have you been mistreated? Are you currently feeling slighted or that God is overlooking the facts of your innocence in an unjust scenario? Can you remember a time in which you felt this way? I could easily write about my husband's current work situation. Your homework is to write about a time in your life when it would have been acceptable, according to the world, to withhold forgiveness. As you are writing, ask God to reveal Himself to you and draw you near to Him so You can understand His great love for you ... even in times of trouble.

Week 3 · Day 14

Day 15: Forgiveness and God's Unusual Request

osea: *Forgiving out of obedience*

Sometimes we simply have to obey. Not ask questions. Not pause to analyze the situation-blind obedience. That way of thinking is not a popular notion in today's society, especially for women.

When my boys were little they enjoyed sing-alongs. We would break out into song in the car, while grocery shopping, or even on the way to school. Now that they are teenagers they do not find it amusing when I begin to sing and try to prod them to join me. One of our favorite songs was the "Obedience song:"

Obedience is,

the very best way,

to show that you believe.

Doing,

exactly,

as the Lord commands.

Doing,

it happily.

Obedience is,

the very best way,

to show that you believe.

O...B....E...D....I...E...N...C...E

Boom, boom, boom!

Oh, we had such fun singing that song. We would always turn about the room during the, "boom, boom, boom" part. I also liked that song because the boys would remember its lyrics when their father or I would remind them to obey a house rule (Like, "Don't hit your brother with your spaghetti!")

That song is the theme of today's devotion. Jesus had a lot to say about forgiveness. "Therefore I tell you, whatever you ask for in prayer, believe that you have received it, and it will be yours. And when you stand praying, if you hold anything against anyone, forgive him, so that your Father in heaven may _____ ." (Mark 11:24-25; NIV).

When Peter asked Jesus how often he should forgive, Jesus told him, "… seventy-seven times" (Matthew 18:22b). Then Jesus stressed the need to offer forgiveness through the poignant parable of the unforgiving servant (Matthew 18:23-35).

Fill in the blanks to the basic outline of this parable.

- King asks his servant to pay back the 10,000 talents (about $18 million)
- Servant cannot pay _____
- King orders that the servant, the servant's wife, kids and land be _____ (verse 25)
- Servant begs for patience and time to repay the loan
- King takes pity and _____ the debt (verse 27)
- Servant leaves the king and finds a fellow servant who owes him money (about $20)
- King's servant begins to _____ his fellow servant (verse 28b)
- Fellow servant _____ for patience and time to repay the loan (verse 29)
- King's servant throws fellow servant in _____ (verse 30)
- King finds out and throws this servant in jail until he _____ (verse 34)

Week 3 · Day 15

Jesus ends this parable by stating, "This is how my heavenly Father will treat each of you unless you forgive your brother from your heart" (verse 35).

The last three words are powerful. "From your heart" means that our mouths cannot utter forgiveness and expect God to check it off His "to do list." He expects forgiveness to be given from our hearts, which is not an easy task!

The beginning of the book of Hosea paints a perfect example of how we must sometimes go through the motions of forgiveness and love, out of obedience to God, and pray that the correct emotion will someday follow.

Read Hosea 1:2.

Who did God tell Hosea to marry? _____

How would you have responded? _____

Now read Hosea 3:1-3.

Hosea had to buy his wife back! In verse 2 it states, "So I bought her for fifteen shekels of silver. …." He then proceeds to tell her that she is not allowed to prostitute herself out anymore and she is to live with him.

All I can say is, "Oh my!" I don't like to share my husband with the TV. Seriously, I actually get jealous of an inanimate object. It is a good thing Jesus didn't tell me I have to forgive our TV. I cannot imagine forgiveness of that level. Yet, as absurd as this example may seem, God forgave us even though we entered an adulterous relationship with the world. He continues to forgive us when we stray from our first love and begin to chase after money, fame, the perfect body … He is *always faithful* to forgive.

Hosea's story is sad but powerful. I challenge you to remember it the next time you feel God is leading you to forgive someone. This story has made me realize that sometimes I must simply obey Him … even if I don't feel like it at the time. God is good. Eventually He will supply the emotion — in this life or the next one.

Your Homework:

Take this time to thank your Heavenly Father for all He has forgiven in your life. Seriously, make a list. Then ask Him to open your eyes to items you may have missed. The next time you feel prompted to forgive, picture this list in your mind and begin to go through the motions of offering forgiveness.

Part II:

Dressing Like a Princess

Week 4

Day 16: Wearing a Mouthguard

One of the scariest movies I can remember being forced to watch was titled "When a Stranger Calls." Please know that I would never purposefully watch anything scary; my family quickly changes the channel if a commercial for a scary movie begins to play. However, my older sister Luanne appeared to find great enjoyment in making me watch scary movies. It makes me sad to think about the demons that must have latched on to her at such a young age. Regardless, if my memory is correct, this particular movie is about a teenage girl who keeps getting strange calls when she is babysitting. This poor girl tries everything to ignore the phone calls but finally decides to call the police. The scariest part of the movie is when the police call to tell her, "Get out of the house … he has been calling you from inside the house." My heart is pounding simply typing these words. I still feel bad for that poor girl. I honestly could not tell you what happened next because Luanne could not get me to take my hands away from my eyes or stop me from singing "Jesus loves me this I know, for the Bible tells me so" as loud as I could.

I am afraid that scary story takes place within every girl's life. All of us have to protect ourselves from a "monster" that can easily destroy everything we love, respect, and have worked diligently to build. The scariest aspect to this monster is that it really is in our house. The monster I speak of is our tongue. James 3:3-12 (The Message) explicitly depicts this very monster:

> *³ A bit in the mouth of a horse controls the whole horse. ⁴⁻⁵ A small rudder on a huge ship in the hands of a skilled captain sets a course in the face of the strongest winds. A word out of your mouth may seem of no account, but it can accomplish nearly anything — or destroy it!*
>
> *⁶ It only takes a spark, remember, to set off a forest fire. A careless or wrongly placed word out of your mouth can do that. By our speech we can ruin the world, turn harmony to chaos, throw mud on a reputation, send the whole world up in smoke and go up in smoke with it, smoke right from the pit of hell.*
>
> *⁷⁻⁸ This is scary: You can tame a tiger, but you can't tame a tongue — it's never been done. The tongue runs wild, a wanton killer. ⁹ With our tongues we bless God our Father, with the same tongues we curse the very men and women He made in his image. ¹⁰ Curses and blessings out of the same mouth!*
>
> *My friends, this can't go on. ¹¹ A spring doesn't gush fresh water one day and brackish the next, does it? ¹² Apple trees don't bear strawberries, do they? Raspberry bushes don't bear apples, do they? You're not going to dip into a polluted mud hole and get a cup of clear, cool water, are you?*

Reread verse 6 and write all the dangers of our speech:

_____
_____
_____
_____

Don't these descriptions sound evil!

In fact, the reason I chose The Message translation of these verses is the way verses 7-8 depict the tongue. According to these verses, the tongue runs wild, a _____.

Now do you believe me when I say you have a monster that has taken up residence within your very mouth?!

Today's devotion will help God's pretty princesses learn how to purchase and set into place their protective mouthguards. My sons' football mouthguards were created to protect their teeth from the giant football players aimed at inflicting pain upon them. Our princess mouthguards are special; this apparatus is created to tame the beast within our mouths and protect the people who come into contact with us. I like to think of my mouthguard as a heavenly invisible fence, similar to the fences that keep dogs in by using a beeping sound to alert them they are wandering too close to the border and then providing a small shock when they ignore the warnings and proceed toward the fence.

Purchasing a Princess Mouthguard

Okay, girls, are you ready to go shopping for your mouthguard? I hope so because you are going to have to stop at several locations to acquire all the parts and pieces that go into making your heavenly invisible fence.

God's Mall

Tina's Tongue Paste Shop
300 flavors
Today's special blend = caramel/peanut butter
The same paste used by King David

→ **James 1:19** → Tongue paste is an important part of the mouthguard because the sticky substance stops you from _____ too quickly and forces you to _____ before you speak!

Wanda's Wonderful World of Words
The largest stock in the world of words spoken directly from God's very mouth!

→ **Matt. 4:4** → Jesus said, "Man does not live on bread alone, but on every _____ that comes from the _____ of _____."

→ **Jer. 15:16** → "When your words came, I _____ them: they were my _____ and my heart's delight."

→ **Prov. 2:6** → "For the Lord gives wisdom, and from his _____ come knowledge and understanding."

↓ **Prov. 30:5** → "Every _____ of God is flawless; he is a _____ to those who take refuge in him."

Saving Grace
Memory Store
Sale today on vivid memory of personal

→ **2 Cor. 5:17** → "Therefore, if anyone is in Christ, he is a new _____; the old is gone, the _____ has come!"

→ **1 Peter 2:24** → "He himself bore our sins in his body on the tree, so that we might die to sins and live for _____; by his _____ you have been _____."

Are you tired from our shopping trip? Let's take an inventory of our great purchases: tongue paste, words spoken from the mouth of God, and the vivid recollection of the great cost and free gift of our salvation. Now that you have purchased the mouthguard items, you must practice setting them all in place.

Your Homework:

Read this prayer and then pray it out loud.

Father, the Bible tells me that the tongue is untamable. But You are able to do anything. I ask You to make my tongue pasty when I want to speak more than I listen. I beg You to create a dry feeling in my mouth that will remind me of Your calling in my life to listen more than I speak. You can create this physical reaction that will help train me to take control over my words. Father God, You are the great Wordsmith. You have the perfect words for every situation. I ask You to help me store Your words in my heart and retrieve them to share with the world. Thank You for the gift of my salvation. I beg You, I implore You, I beseech You to help me remember the great cost that was paid and my obligation to honor the family name. Please don't let my words bring You shame! In the precious name of Jesus I make these requests.

I am going to ask you to pray this prayer every day this week. I can promise you that God is faithful; He will allow you to begin to gain control of the beast that lurks within your mouth. Think of sweet Esther and her control over her tongue. What would have happened if she didn't obey her uncle and had told people about her nationality (Esther 2:20)?

_____
_____
_____

Day 17: Using God's Mouthwash

We live in a fallen world. The days of the Garden of Eden are so far removed from our current lives they are more like a fairy tale than a possibility. As a result, each and every one of us will sin. Our words can hurt people, even when it was never our intent to cause harm. According to the Bible, here are a few of the ways our mouth can cause us to sin:

Evil	Curses	Destruction	Deceit
Slander	Wicked	Bitterness	Lies

Choose words from the list above to complete the following sentences.

Psalm 10:7 states: "His mouth is full of _____ and _____ and threats; trouble and evil are under his tongue."

Psalm 50:19-20 states: "You use your mouth for _____ and harness your tongue to _____. You speak continually against your brother and _____ your own mother's son."

Psalm 52:2 states, "Your tongue plots _____; it is like a sharpened razor, you who practice deceit."

Isaiah 59:3b states, "Your lips have spoken lies, your tongue mutters _____ things."

Romans 3:13 states, "Their throats are open graves; their tongues practice deceit. The poison of vipers in on their lips. Their mouths are full of cursing and _____."

In other words, our mouths can easily become "dirty" from the words we use or the manner in which we say them.

For example, I could take the phrase "nice dress" and use it as a compliment or sarcastic response. The compliment would arise by me smiling at a student and saying, "nice dress." The student would leave feeling good about her outfit. I could also use that same phrase to cause harm simply by changing my tone to a sarcastic one that would imply, "Who in her right mind would wear that dress in public?"

It is not always our words that cause us to sin; sarcasm and coarse joking are also ways in which we can easily "dirty" our royal mouths!

All of us will need to rinse out our mouths with God's heavenly mouthwash.

Has your mouth been infected?

- Gossip
- Lies
- Excessive Words
- Quick Responses Without Thought
- Sarcastic Tones
- Poor Humor
- Cursing
- Negativity
- Deception
- False Flattery

Clean it with...

God's Mouthwash

Product Disclaimer—This product will only work if it is applied promptly and consistently when the mouth becomes dirtied.

Ingredients: fear, sorrow, confession, submission, blood

Week 4 · Day 17

Did you read the ingredients? It is always a good idea to read the ingredients before you buy a product. For example, what do you think these ingredients make: corn syrup, sugar, dextrose, modified corn starch, water, gelatin, tetrasodium pyrophaosphate, artificial flavor, and artificial color? Circle the item you think has these ingredients: syrup, candy cane, frosting, or marshmallow. If you circled the last item, you are correct. I cannot believe how much sugar is in one very innocent-looking food item (no wonder I like them)!

Your Homework:

So what are the ingredients in God's mouthwash? List them here:

1. _____
2. _____
3. _____
4. _____
5. _____

Is this a product you would buy? Seriously, is there anything about this product that sounds yummy and worth spending your money on so you can "swirl it around in your mouth" on a daily basis?

Write your reaction to these ingredients.

_____
_____
_____
_____
_____
_____

I believe our honest reaction to these ingredients is why we often go around with dirtied mouths. God's mouthwash is not chocolate flavored; it is not sweet to the taste. His cleansing process is painful and requires sacrifice on our part. It is no wonder we refrain from cleansing our mouths! Tomorrow you are going to spend a great deal of time exploring each of the ingredients. End today by praying the "mouth prayer" again (from Day 16). It is okay if you begin to add your own words as you communicate with your Father.

Day 18: Washing Your Mouth with Fear and Sorrow?

Today your job is to dig in deep into each of the ingredients in order to understand these five essential elements and include them in your daily efforts to clean the sins of the mouth.

1. Fear (Specifically, the fear of the Lord)

Complete the following verses:

Proverbs 1:7a "The fear of the Lord is the _____ of _____ ..."

Psalm 19:9 "The fear of the Lord is _____ ... ")

2 Corinthians 7:1b "... let us cleanse ourselves from everything that can defile our body or spirit. And let us work toward complete purity because _____ God (NLT)."

What is meant by fear? Should we fear God like I fear bad people or snakes or heights? Should my pulse begin to raise, my body break out in a cold sweat, and my legs freeze in fear ... like my body reacts to heights? No! I cannot emphasize that answer enough.

The word "fear" in Proverbs 1:7 is "Yir'ah" in the Hebrew and it means "reverence" (Strong's Concordance).

One of my favorite vocabulary strategies is word mapping. I like this strategy because it allows the learner to turn a relatively unknown word into a known and used word.

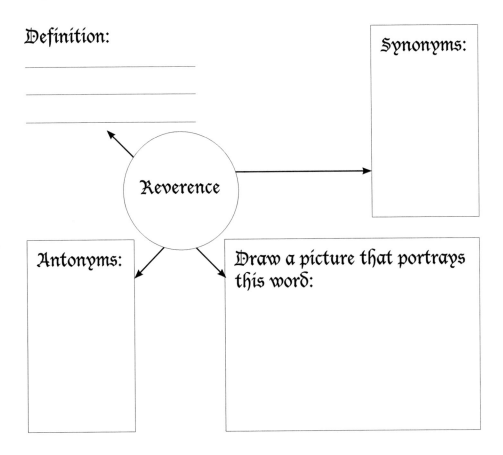

I especially like how John MacArthur explains the fear of God: "The fear of the Lord is a state of mind in which one's own attitudes, will, feelings, deeds and goals are exchanged for God's (The MacArthur Bible Commentary, p. 699)."

I would like to illustrate this transference of thinking and behaviors due to a reverent attitude through a family story. As you know, I have two teenage boys who adore their daddy. Really, I think they still believe Ray can walk on water. One of Ray's attributes is he is the same man regardless of his audience. Countless people have told my boys and me that they appreciate the fact that Ray is a "what you see is what you get" kind of man. One day one of my sons called me at work and asked me to pick him up from school. I was completely disoriented because he said he wasn't sick or in trouble; he said he needed to talk to me. Upon arriving at school he entered my car and immediately embraced me and began to cry. Please try to picture this scene. My teenage boy, who outweighs me by almost a hundred pounds, is leaning over and sobbing. I haven't even put the car in park yet. He then proceeds to tell me that he has been living a double life. Now I am terrified. Does he mean he is selling drugs, having sex, stealing cars? My mind is racing a hundred miles a minute. I finally put the car in park and asked him to pray with me. I believe I needed that prayer more than he did. After he finished crying, he begas to explain to me that he has been smoking and cussing when he is around his friends and behaving like the "clean-cut Christian boy" when he is around us. He explains that he wants to live like his dad; be the same young man no matter who is around him. Now I am crying. I am amazed by God's great love for my family. My husband is not perfect; I have a lot of stories to prove this point. However, I believe this story illustrates how we should fear, or show reverence, to our Father. It is out of great respect that we should be careful about what we say. That same attitude of respect, awe, reference and fear should bring us great sorrow when we realize we have used our words in a manner that are not pleasing to Him.

2. Sorrow

Sadness, grief, regret, distress, unhappiness and mourning are all synonyms for sorrow. I believe we will experience varying degrees of sorrow as we grow to know our Father. Think of this aspect in personal terms. Please fill in the following blanks with one of the synonyms for sorrow.

You were telling a friend how ugly that *stranger's* outfit was when you realize she heard you. _____

You were telling a friend how ugly your *boss's* outfit was when you realize she heard you. _____

You were telling a friend how ugly your *sister's* outfit was when you realize she heard you. _____

You were telling a friend how ugly your *mom's* outfit was when you realize she heard you. _____

You were telling a friend how ugly *Beth Moore's* outfit was when you realize she heard you. (Beth Moore, a well-known evangelist, author and teacher, would be my "spiritual giant" pick, but you can put in another name if you like. My mom would probably put Kay Arthur here.)

_____

Okay, here are my responses and explanations to those same statements.

(Stranger=unhappy) I would be unhappy that I hurt that person's feelings.

(Boss=regret) I would regret saying something that hurt my boss and could hurt my job.

(Sister=sadness) I would feel sad because my sister's eyes would look sad, especially if it was my sister Carrie.

(Mom=distress) I would be distressed because I know that God tells me to honor my mother and I would have hurt Him with my words … along with offending my mom.

(Beth Moore=mourning) Wow, I believe I would go into mourning if this instance occurred. I adore Beth Moore. I have learned so much about my Father because of her work. I would be so full of sorrow that it would probably take Beth Moore asking me to forgive myself to get out of it. I respect, admire, adore and have a high opinion of this woman.

Can you see how our sorrow shifted depending on our relationship to the person we offended? I believe that is why 2 Corinthians 7:10-11a states, "Godly sorrow brings repentance that leads to salvation and leaves no regret, but worldly sorrow brings death. See what this godly sorrow has produced in you: what earnestness, what eagerness to clear yourselves ..." The sad truth is that we cannot even feel the proper level of sorrow without the prompting of the Holy Spirit. The second part of that verse, "to clear yourselves," will be explored in tomorrow's devotion.

Your Homework:

Think about a time in your life where you experienced true, gut-wrenching sorrow. Take a few minutes to write about that experience; make sure you include the emotions you were feeling and how your body physically responded to this occurrence.

_____

_____

_____

_____

_____

_____

Can you imagine how close we would be to God if our body and emotions reacted in this same fashion when we realized we had said something that was not pleasing to Him? Wow, I believe our words would be few because we would be extremely careful not to go through that kind of suffering and sorrow too frequently!

Don't forget to end today with the mouth prayer.

Day 19: Washing Your Mouth with Confession, Submission, and Blood

Yesterday you explored the areas of fear and sorrow — two critical ingredients in God's mouthwash. Today you will be digging into the Bible to understand the last three ingredients: confession, submission and blood.

Confession—Coming from a good Italian home, with a strong Roman Catholic influence, I have a vivid picture of confession. A priest sits behind a wall and one person goes in to confess his/her sins. If my memory serves right, that person says some Hail Marys and goes on with his/her life. I remember thinking "What changed?" My cousins would immediately begin lying, cussing and drinking once they left church.

So what exactly is confession? We know that reverence for God should lead us to feel sorrow over an error. That sorrow should direct us to confess because according to I John 1:9, "If we confess our sins, He is faithful and just and will forgive us our sins and purify us from all unrighteousness." I like the notion of being forgiven and purified, don't you? But what does confession entail?

Let's take a look at the man that God called, "a man after His own heart" —David (I Samuel 13:14)—and how he went about confessing his sins.

The story line is that David committed adultery with Bathsheba and then murdered her husband to cover his transgression. The prophet, Nathan, has been sent by God to let David know that his sins have not been hidden from God.

2 Samuel 12:13: "Then David said to Nathan, 'I have sinned against the Lord.'"

Our next story begins with David ordering a census without consulting God. His actions could have been to use the army to pursue more land than the Lord had given him or merely to allow David to glory in the size of his army. Either possibility was against God's will. As a result,

> "David was conscience-stricken after he had counted the fighting men, and he said to the Lord, 'I have sinned greatly in what I have done. Now, O Lord, I beg you, take away the guilt of your servant. I have done a very foolish thing'" (2 Samuel 24:10).

How did David react in both instances? He said, I have _____ against _____ _____. Those words are powerful because David is claiming responsibility for his actions and acknowledging who he really offended.

Ray always tells my boys, "Don't mess up an apology with an excuse!" I believe this saying has biblical merit because God desires for us to claim our errors, without providing a plethora of excuses, and admit that we have hurt Him in the process.

Let me make this point personal. Pretend that I have just run into the back of your foot with my grocery cart (which is a painful occurrence). Circle the apology you would prefer:

A. "Oh, my, I am so sorry I hit you with my cart. I couldn't see you because you were partially hidden with other groceries and you were talking on your cell phone."

B. "Oh, my, I am so sorry I hit you with my cart. I was talking on my cell phone and looking for the cheese and certainly did not mean to hurt you."

C. "Oh, my, I am so sorry I hit you with my cart. I can see that I truly hurt your foot. What can I do to bring you some comfort? Would you like to sit down for a bit?"

The first two had a different tone, right? The last one followed David's pattern of confession: admission and acknowledgement.

Submission—Okay, see if you can fill in these blanks. The fear of God should lead us to _____ and that uncomfortable feeling should cause us to _____ . (Did you fill in "sorrow" and "confess"? I sure hope so.) The next ingredient in God's mouthwash is submission; a word that is often unpopular among women due to the world's perception of the word.

So what is submission? Please turn to James 4:7&10 and fill in the blanks:

"_____ *yourselves, then, to God. Resist the* _____ *and he will flee from you.* _____ *yourselves before the Lord, and He will* _____ *you* _____ ."

As they say here in the South, "Wooooooweeee, y'all!" Now sisters, does submission sound bad to you?! According to this God-inspired Scripture, my submission to God results in the devil fleeing and God lifting me up. I think I want to be the "submission queen". But we still haven't discovered what God means by "submit".

The Greek word for submit is "hupotasso" which means to be subordinate, under obedience, or to submit self unto. These words usually ruffle some of us girls' feathers. Do we really want to be "under obedience"? Yes, yes, and oh yes, is my answer to that question. Think of it this way. You can only serve one master. You must choose God or the devil. Lack of a choice defers you to the devil. I don't know about you, girls, but I want to be on the winning team and according to Jesus, that is God's team (John 16:33b)! So submission means that we line up under God's authority and follow His lead. I like that thought.

Think of it this way. I don't really like crowds. In fact, I tend to become a bit frightened when the mass of people begin closing in on me (I know; God did not give me a spirit of fear. He is still working on me). That is why I usually go with Ray—my darling husband is 6'3 and 285 pounds. He walks in front of me and makes this "magic bubble" of comfort. I don't get bumped into or pushed around. It is a wonderful way to travel through crowds. I picture my Heavenly Father being very willing to perform this same task in my every endeavor; it is me that forgets to line myself up behind Him and then follow.

Submission is a key ingredient in God's cleansing mouthwash because if we leave confession without submitting ourselves daily (sometimes by the hour for me) to God, we will end up getting run over by the crowd, losing our temper, saying something inappropriate, and then, bam, we are right back confessing again. Submission provides the protection of our heavenly Father—don't leave home without it!

I believe King David was talking about the act of submission when he wrote, "The sacrifices of God are a broken spirit; a broken and contrite heart, O God, you will not despise" (Psalm 51: 17). It is when we are broken that we are most willing to align ourselves behind the protective shadow of our Heavenly Father!

The blood of Jesus—he final ingredient is critical. I am so thankful that I don't have to go into my backyard and kill a sheep or ox, or anything for that matter. The blood of Jesus creates this strange dichotomy of emotions: I am sad that Jesus had to suffer and die and incredibly happy for the gift of salvation. Regardless of my emotions, Jesus is our great mediator. The Bible states, "For there is one God and one mediator between God and men, the man Christ Jesus" (I Timothy 2:5). It also depicts the power of the blood of Jesus: "How much more, then, will the blood of Christ, who through the eternal Spirit offered Himself unblemished to God, cleanse our consciences from acts that lead to death, so that we may serve the living God" (Hebrews 9:14)! We cannot achieve anything clean without the blood of Jesus. I John 1:7 clearly states this fact: "But if we walk in the light, as He is in the light, we have fellowship with one another, and the blood of Jesus, His Son, purifies us from all sin."

Your Homework:

Today I am going to ask you to complete a memory activity. This activity is geared to assist you in remembering all five components in God's mouthwash.

The acronym for these components is FSCSB (Fear, Sorrow, Confession, Submission, Blood). Your job is to come up with a fun way to remember these important words. Write your technique here:

_____
_____
_____
_____
_____
_____
_____
_____

Don't forget to say our mouth prayer again. Have you been blessed with an unexplainable dry mouth yet?

Week 4 · Day 19

Day 20: Family, Friends, and Fellowship? Can These Three Items Work Together?

The Bible clearly tells us to honor our parents (Matthew 15:4) and be kind one to another (I Thessalonians 5:15). My question is, "When is it acceptable to back away from family and friends who don't listen and always bring drama into my life?" If you have no idea what I am talking about, you should hit your knees and immediately begin praising God for protecting you from family and friend drama! Please use today's devotional as a means of encouraging and supporting people in your life who do encounter daily dramas.

My birth family has tremendous power to hurt me. Unkind words, gossip, lies, and sad stories are the basic conversations that occur when we talk. In fact, Niko (my youngest son) stated on our last trip to see my family, "Mom, it seems like you gossip when you are with your family." Those words hit me like a brick wall. Do I gossip? I thought I was merely "venting" with my sister about our family woes. But, was my venting really a means of talking about other people in my family?

Ray would like nothing better than for me to walk away and forget they have phones or where they live. My poor husband has watched them hurt me, intentionally, on too many occasions. My fear has always been that this action would interfere with my relationship with God. Recently, my family, one by one, called on the same day and literally tore me down. By the end of the day I was crying and praying and of no use to Ray and the boys. All three of my boys asked me, again, to protect myself from these interactions. My response was, "Please show me in the Bible where it says it is okay to walk away from family/friends just because they are not kind." They began praying and searching and enlisting the help of my in-laws.

My time in God's Word is what finally answered this question. I pray that this discovery will be a blessing to my sisters in Christ as you encounter difficult and unkind family members and friends. God brought me to 2 Timothy 2:14-26. Please slowly read through these verses:

> [14] Keep reminding them of these things. Warn them before God against quarreling about words; it is of no value, and only ruins those who listen. [15] Do your best to present yourself to God as one approved, a workman who does not need to be ashamed and who correctly handles the word of truth. [16] Avoid godless chatter, because those who indulge in it will become more and more ungodly. [17] Their teaching will spread like gangrene. Among them are Hymenaeus and Philetus, [18] who have wandered away from the truth. They say that the resurrection has already taken place, and they destroy the faith of some. [19] Nevertheless, God's solid foundation stands firm, sealed with this inscription: 'The Lord knows those who are his,' and, 'Everyone who confesses the name of the Lord must turn away from wickedness.'
>
> [20] In a large house there are articles not only of gold and silver, but also of wood and clay; some are for noble purposes and some for ignoble. [21] If a man cleanses himself from the latter, he will be an instrument for noble purposes, made holy, useful to the Master and prepared to do any good work.
>
> [22] Flee the evil desires of youth, and pursue righteousness, faith, love and peace, along with those who call on the Lord out of a pure heart. [23] Don't have anything to do with foolish and stupid arguments, because you know they produce quarrels. [24] And the Lord's servant must not quarrel; instead, he must be kind to everyone, able to teach, not resentful. [25] Those who oppose him he must gently instruct, in the hope that God will grant them repentance leading them to a knowledge of the truth, [26] and that they will come to their senses and escape from the trap of the devil, who has taken them captive to do his will."

Interesting reading, right! Now, please take a highlighter and accent the information in these verses that addresses our speech: verses 14, 15, 16, 19, 23 and 24.

Verse 14 warns us against _____ about words.

Verse 15 reminds us to correctly handle the _____ of truth.

Verse 16 tells us to avoid _____ _____!

Verse 19 states that if we confess the name of _____ _____ we must turn away from _____.

Verse 23 informs us to have nothing to do with _____ and _____ arguments, because they cause _____.

Verse 24 clearly states that the Lord's princess must not _____.

Oh my, the majority of my conversations with my family, and troubled friends, have been about "godless chatter" and arguing over words — either spoken by us or others. God clearly tells His own to avoid, resist, refrain from these acts of speech. In fact, reread verse 16 and complete this formula: godless chatter=less _____. I hate the idea that my useless conversations could result in me becoming less like God; however, this train of thought makes perfect sense. I cannot imagine the Holy Spirit enjoying or being enriched by me listening to my sisters tell me how horrible our mom is about something .... or listening to my mom talk about how unkind my sisters are about something. But God does not tell us to ignore them. No, He tells us in verse 25 to _____ instruct them in order for God (not you or me) to lead them to the knowledge of the truth. The Scripture goes on to explain (verse 26) how they are trapped by _____.

I have offered biblical advice on countless occasions. This advice has been ignored and the pattern of sin continues in my birth family. I always thought it was my job to listen and repeat this pattern in the hopes that one day they would let God into their lives. However, I am beginning to understand that my time with them is hurting my relationship with God because I am engaging in and/or listening to speech that is not pleasing to Him. Verse 17 states that the teachings of those we spend our time with will eventually spread like _____, which is a horrible and deadly disease. I remember my pastor once standing on a chair to show me how hard it is for him to pick someone up to his level. He strained and pulled and made a great effort. He was a football player trying to pick up a small man. Then the man gave a tug and our pastor came falling down. We all laughed, but his point was well made. The time we spend with people, and the conversations we enter, affect us … either for the positive or negative.

Verses 20 and 21 talk about different categories of people. Sisters, God makes it clear that we are expected to be His _____ and silver; instruments created for noble purposes and useful to our _____.

Please don't think that I'm saying it is okay to write people off when they have troubles or worries they need to share with you. I am merely suggesting that we follow God's lead and "gently instruct" them about God's abilities and desire to assist them and then let God lead. If these people consistently refrain from following biblical advice and are causing your mouth and/or ears to sin, then "flee" from them and "pursue righteousness … along with those who call on the Lord out of a pure heart." Did you notice the last part of that verse? God is telling us to spend time with our sisters in Christ and build each other up.

Your Homework:

Reflect on the topics of conversation that occur between you and your friends, family, colleagues. Write the basic ideas for these topics and then put the words "God approved" or "avoid" next to them. Then pray and ask God to open your eyes to areas in your life that may need to be turned over to Him while you step back and let Him work. Sometimes God may equip us to help our friends and family like Isaiah 50:4, "The Sovereign Lord has given me an instructed tongue, to know the word that sustains the weary … ."

Don't forget to say our mouth prayer one more time.

Father, the Bible tells me that the tongue is untamable. But You are the able to do anything. I ask You to make my tongue pasty when I want to speak more than I listen. I beg You to create a dry feeling in my mouth that will remind me of Your calling in my life to listen more than I speak. You can create this physical reaction that will help train me to take control over my words. Father God, You are the great Word Smith. You have the perfect words for every situation. I ask You to help me store Your words in my heart and retrieve them to share with the world. Thank You for the gift of my salvation. I beg You, I implore You, I beseech You to help me remember the great cost that was paid and my obligation to honor the family name. Please don't let my words bring You shame! In the precious name of Jesus I make these requests.

Week 5

Day 21: Applying the Perfect Brightening Serum (The Art of Worship)

Children can be brutally honest. I had been a classroom teacher for over a decade when I decided to leave the classroom to help fourth- and fifth-grade students who had been held back a year and were in danger of another retention if they could not pass the Florida state reading test. These economically poor, but street-smart children caused me to spend a lot of time praying and teaching to earn their trust. The first month of school passed with them entering the room, going through the motions of my requests, and leaving with blank looks on their faces. But God is so good to me, and soon their faces began to reflect hope and trust. That is when they started talking to me about their fears and hopes. This trust also brought about their willingness to ask me questions. One day, as I was helping Shay (one of my most resistant learners), she looked at me and asked, "How come your face has all those lines, Dr. Jones? Is that a white people thing?" Well, I responded appropriately by having her return to the reading work at hand and telling her it is not proper to ask a woman about her smile wrinkles. I made sure I talked to her with a smile on my face and let her know I cared for her deeply.

Guess what I went shopping for when I left school that day? Yes, for the first time in my life I was looking for magic erase-those-wrinkles-from-my-face cream. I had no idea how many items were available to assist me in my quest for a clear, radiant face (or how expensive these items were)! My favorite skin products were the brightening serums. These creams advertised their ability to change my "dull and dry" face by making it "bright and clear." I liked the sound of "bright and clear." Who wants a "dull and dry face" anyway? My poor husband has been buying me these products for almost a decade now. I can count on getting some every Christmas. I have no idea if they are working, but I sure like to tell myself that my face looks brighter and clearer because I use them.

Dear, sweet sisters, I have good news for all of us. Our Father has the perfect brightening serum recipe. He can make our faces radiate like the bright morning sun! I have proof; read Exodus 34:29 and fill in the blanks.

"When Moses came down from Mount Sinai with the two tablets of the Testimony in his hands, he was not aware that _____ _____ was radiant because he had _____ with the Lord."

Now read Matthew 17:1-2 and complete the blanks.

"After six days Jesus took with him Peter, James and John the brother of James, and led them up a high mountain by themselves. There he was transfigured before them. His _____ shone like the _____, and his cloths became white as the light."

Luke 9:29 recounts this same transfiguration with a different metaphor.

"As he was praying, the appearance of his face changed, and his clothes became as bright as a _____ of _____."

In both instances Moses and Jesus physically pursued God's presence. In fact, they both went to a mountaintop to spend time with God. One of the key ingredients to a brighter face is our *purposeful physical actions to spend time alone with God.* Our Father wants us to pursue Him.

Moses encountered the presence of God when he approached the burning bush (Exodus 3). Moses spoke with God and learned about how he was going to be used to set the Israelites free. However, Moses' face did not shine after this encounter. This meeting was planned and implemented by God. Yes, Moses had to be curious enough to walk over to the burning bush, but his actions were not in pursuit of God.

I want to make this "pursuit of God" personal to you. Imagine you are in love with a wonderful man. Which of the following two scenarios would leave you feeling "dizzy with love?"

Scenario A—Your boyfriend has driven an hour and a half to spend time with you. You know he has worked all day and will have to be up at 5 a.m. the next morning. Yet he stays until 10:30 that night because he thoroughly enjoys spending time with you. You two go to the park, sit on a bench, and talk for hours. He continually looks into your eyes and carefully listens to all you have to say. He laughs at your jokes and feels pain for your inner worries.

Scenario B—You are shopping at the mall when you bump into your boyfriend. He has a list of items that have to be bought (which you don't realize are all for you) so he appears a bit unfocused and preoccupied. You tell him how happy you are to see him and ask him about his day. His answers are short and his eyes frequently glance at his watch.

Yes, we all would prefer scenario A. Now, please think of these scenarios as ways we could spend time with God. *Do we have a special place where we go to meet with Him?* When we are in this place do we totally concentrate on Him, telling Him what is on our hearts and asking Him what is on His heart and mind? Or, do we accidentally "bump into" God at church while we are in Sunday school class, the worship service, small Bible study group or another form of fellowship? Just like scenario B, all of these examples are for God;

Week 5 · Day 21 127

yet, He would rather we stop our moving about and pursue some time to just be with Him.

Sisters, we like to be pursued. We like the feeling of someone loving us so much he will move mountains, and kill dragons, and climb towers to be with the one he loves. Don't you think our Father God, who loves us more than we can comprehend, will feel loved by those same actions?! So, if you want a brighter face—one that reflects God's goodness and grace—pursue Him.

I will end today with one more story. Like many of you, I find myself at Walmart more often than I would like. The store is always busy and the one in West Palm Beach was usually full of grumpy, angry and pushy people. For example, if I left my cart unattended for the briefest moment, it was taken —regardless of what I had already placed in it. I dreaded going to that store; however, feeding two teenage boys—and all their friends—meant that I needed to save money on groceries.

The store had several "greeters" who generally stood at the door and barely made eye contact with people. They appeared as unhappy to be there as I felt. But, there was one woman who was different. I felt oddly drawn to her. She didn't look different than anyone else, yet she had a peculiar "shine" to her. I found myself seeking her face whenever I attended that store. She smiled at everyone, but it wasn't her smile. I couldn't place the feeling she emanated until one day my mother-in-law told me she knew this woman and she was a great woman of faith. Ta da! I now understood. Her great love for God shone like a beacon of light in a dark and dreary store. Ladies, God's light can, and will, shine on our faces!

Your Homework:

Many great men and women of faith had specific areas they would go to in order to spend time with God. One of my favorite stories is of a man of God whose prayer closet had two worn spots in the carpet from the years of him kneeling there in the presence of God. I bet his children never replaced that carpet!

Where can you go to be alone with God? Women, this question is not easy. Satan likes to keep us busy. In fact, busyness is one of my biggest sins. Today I want you to pray and ask God to help you find the perfect place to run to meet Him. Because I have been a mom for 16 years, the closet is a good place for me. I can close the door and hit my knees and be alone with Him. As a child I would hide in the closet from the trials of my family — God was always there with me. As an adult I should run to the closet to be with Him because I miss and love Him. I also like to go on hikes with God. Just me and my Father!

Write your plan here:

Day 22: Choosing the Right Lipstick

Yesterday we spent time exploring God's ability to make our faces shine in a dark and dreary world. Today we are going to learn how to apply lipstick that is pleasing to our Father and will make the world wonder, "Where can I buy that shade of lipstick?"

Aren't you amazed by the tenderness of our Father? I picture our Heavenly Father taking the time to walk down the cosmetics aisle with us and discuss the different shades of color and what each color portrays to the world. This visual picture makes my heart smile. My earthly father wanted boys, so he didn't discuss makeup unless he was yelling, "What is all this ^&*%%*^ in the bathroom!" You may not have had a father with such colorful speech and a short temper; yet, I am guessing not many of your fathers took the time to talk about lipstick with you. (If they did, girl, you better hit your knees right now and praise God for giving you a daddy with that kind of tender heart!)

Which shade will you wear right now?

Pink=Applying Encouragement—Pink makes me feel happy. The bright and cheery shade brings a smile to my face. It would appear that marketing companies have discovered that many women react in this same fashion. Have you noticed the new pink baking pans, cooking utensils, and electronics? Hmmm, a pink TV … I like it!

Our Father wants us to remember to put on our pink lipstick and encourage one another.

Read and fill in the blanks to these verses:

I Thessalonians 4:17-18: "*After that, we who are still alive and are left will be caught up together with them in the clouds to meet the Lord in the air. And so we will be with the Lord forever. Therefore _____ _____ _____ with these words.*"

We are to encourage our brothers and sisters in Christ!

I Thessalonians 5:14: *"And we urge you, brothers (and sisters), warn those who are idle, encourage _____ _____, help the weak, be patient with everyone."*

We are to encourage our Christian brothers and sisters to live boldly for Christ!

Titus 1:9: *"He must hold firmly to the trustworthy message as it has been taught, so that he can encourage others by _____ _____ and refute those who oppose it."*

We are to encourage others with the truth of the scriptures!

Titus 2:6: *"Similarly, encourage the young men (women) to be _____."*

We are to encourage each other by modeling personal restraint and control over our tongue and actions!

Hebrews 3:13: *"But encourage one another _____, as long as it is called Today, so that none of you may be hardened by _____ _____."* The Message translation brings this verse into today's terminology: *"For as long as it's still God's Today, keep each other on your toes so sin doesn't slow down your reflexes."*

Week 5 · Day 22

We are to encourage each other daily by strengthening our spiritual muscles through rigorous prayer and discussions about God's Word!

Golden Toffee=Applying Empathy—Unlike red and pink, a light brown shade can be worn in almost any situation. I probably wouldn't wear red or pink lipstick to a funeral, but I would feel comfortable applying a soft brown color. This shade implies warmth and neutrality. Our Father wants us to wear this shade when we must bear each others' burdens.

A colleague at Liberty University just lost her 46-year old-husband. My heart hurts for her. I cannot imagine going through one day without my husband. The worst thing I could do to my colleague is shun her out of my awkward feelings and fear of not saying the right words. I would like to share a painful memory to help illustrate this point.

Ray and I had been married for a year and a half when I discovered I was pregnant. We were excited and scared. We made plans and talked about the pregnancy with our friends at church and work. Then I miscarried in my fifth month. I remember every detail of those two days. The worst part, though, was the feeling of isolation. My friends appeared to avoid me. Conversations quickly changed when I walked into a room. I felt alone and confused. Many years later I asked a few of them why they reacted in that manner. A good friend said, "Oh, Jill, I felt so guilty that I was pregnant and you lost your baby. I figured the last person you would want to be around was me. I was also a bit afraid to talk about the subject." I understood what she was thinking; however, I believe she was buying Satan's ugly lies. I needed her to be there for me and just listen or cry with me.

Ladies, we must ask our Father to show us how to be sensitive to each other and when to apply our golden toffee lipstick.

Jesus demonstrated great empathy on more than one occasion.

Matthew 9:35-36 "Jesus went through all the towns and villages, teaching in their synagogues, preaching the good news of the kingdom

and healing every disease and sickness. When he saw the crowds, he _____ on them, because they were harassed and helpless, like sheep without a shepherd."

Matthew 11:28 "Come to me, all you who are weary and burdened, and I will _____ _____ _____."

John 11:33-35 "When Jesus saw her weeping, and the Jews who had come along with her also weeping, he was deeply moved in spirit and troubled. 'Where have you laid him?' he asked. 'Come and see, Lord,' they replied. Jesus _____."

Jesus is our example. He felt the pain of those around Him. He shared in their misery and suffering. He had to be so tired. Everywhere He went He healed and preached and touched people. I believe His great empathy provided energy to keep moving from town to town and this same ability to feel our pain spurred Jesus to enlist the help of His disciples in Matthew 10:1.

The Holy Spirit lives within us. He can help us understand each others' burdens in order to meet each others' needs. Remember this truth the next time Satan tries to sell you the lie, "What if you say the wrong words or don't know what to say at all?"

Red=Applying Salvation—According to a study in which 98 college students recorded their emotional responses to color, the color red produced an emotional dichotomy: "… the color red prompted both positive and negative emotional reactions. Red was seen to be positive because it was associated with love and romance, while the negative aspects of red included having associations with fight and blood as well as Satan and evil" (Kaya & Epps, 2004, p. 2).

Ladies, we need to apply this color of lipstick very carefully. The color red can lead to a beautiful scenario in which we share the salvation message

Week 5 · Day 22

and lead a dear sister to Jesus Christ and His saving grace. Let us turn to Jesus for the perfect example of tenderly and carefully sharing the need and process of salvation.

Please use the following reading road map to read and respond to John 4:6-15. (Remember, good readers adjust their speed depending on their purpose. Skimming requires you to use your finger and read every other or every third word. Scanning is like the grocery check-out process, your eyes quickly look at the entire text to find one or two words.)

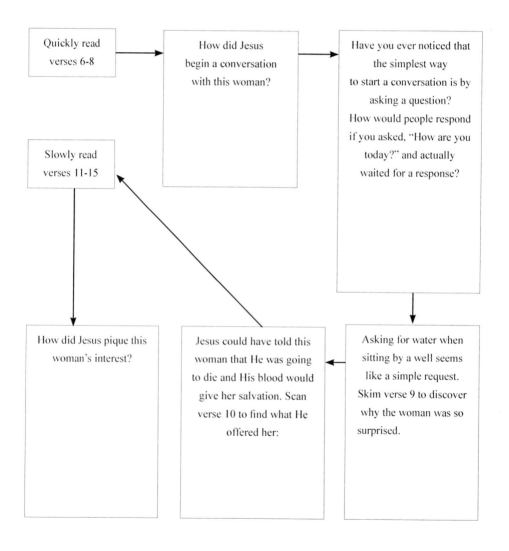

This story ends with many Samaritans believing in Jesus and receiving salvation (John 4:39)! All because Jesus began with a question, talked about a common subject (thirst), and carefully led this woman to the realization that she needed a savior. Our red lipstick can create this warm and positive experience.

Or, it can evoke negative emotions that leave people feeling defensive or on guard. I have heard, and experienced, too many instances of salvation preached from a legalistic perspective. What if Jesus began that same conversation with this question: "Why do you continue to live in sin with men?" Hmmm, that woman would have either turned around quickly and left Jesus alone or become defensive and told Him to mind his own business. Do you see how the salvation message is like people's reactions to the color red: it can incite both positive and negative reactions. I will never forget a teenage boy telling me I was not saved because I listened to secular music. Oooh, he made me mad! I continued to listen to that music just to spite him! Have you ever had an experience with legalism? Write it here in order to help you remember to carefully apply your red lipstick so you don't offend or scare away anyone from Jesus' saving grace!

Lip Gloss=Applying Wisdom—This form of lipstick should be applied regularly, regardless of which shade you may already be wearing. In fact, lip gloss enhances your smile without any color! This crystal clear, shiny substance should remind us girls to apply wisdom to our mouth daily. And to reapply this wisdom when we notice it is wearing off.

Read James 3:17 and fill in the pertinent blanks.

"But the wisdom that comes from heaven is first of all _____ ; then peace-loving, considerate, submissive, full of mercy and good fruit, impartial and sincere."

Proverbs 31:26 reminds us that a woman of noble character "... speaks with wisdom, and faithful _____ is on her tongue."

Your Homework:

Color in each box below and then write how this color of lipstick impacts your outward actions.

Pink	_____ _____ _____

Golden Toffee	_____ _____ _____

Red	_____ _____ _____

Clear	_____ _____ _____

Day 23: Adorable Ears

Be careful little ears what you hear.
Be careful little ears for you hear.
For the Father up above,
is looking down in love.
Oh, be careful little ears what you hear!

I cannot believe God brought that song to mind this many years later. I haven't heard or sung that song since I was a little girl. As a young child I can remember thinking, "Wow, God hears everything I hear … uh oh, I hear some pretty bad stuff in my house." It is amazing what you don't hear from a closet, though. God helped me find the softest, safest, and most sound-resistant hiding spots. I bet God provided some wonderful safe havens for you, too.

As an adult I have often wondered if I would feel safer in a closet. Actually, I often do because I have created a prayer closet. However, God does not want me to live in that closet. In fact, Jesus told us to, "… go and make disciples of all nations, baptizing them in the name of the Father and of the Son and of the Holy Spirit …" (Matthew 28:19).

So, we must actively live in a fallen and desperate world. Our ears are going to hear more than they should. As daughters of The King, we must be prepared to battle the words that are flung our way. Our princess ears have three cleaning mechanisms: God-dipped Q-tips, eardrum music, and blood earrings.

God dipped Q-tips are a means by which we use Scripture to clean the "gunk" out of our ears **before** we allow these words to negatively impact our actions. Jesus portrayed this process beautifully in Matthew 4:1-11.

Please read all 11 verses and complete the following sentences.

Jesus went without food for _____. Satan's first verbal attack was on His apparent physical need. Satan says, "If you are the Son of God, tell these stones to become _____." This task would be easy work for our Lord and Savior. Yet Jesus does not comply with the bully's taunt. Instead, Jesus redirects the argument to Scripture and responds by reminding Satan about Deuteronomy 8:2 & 3. "Remember, how the Lord your God led you all the way in the desert these forty years, to _____ you and to _____ you in order to know what was in your heart, whether or not you would keep his _____ . He humbled you, causing you to hunger and then _____ with manna, which neither you nor your father had known, to _____ that man does not live by bread alone but on every word that comes from the mouth the Lord."

Satan tries a different tactic now. Please read Psalm 91:11-12. Now re-read Matthew 4:6. Satan is actually using God's words to challenge our Jesus. However, Satan is misusing scripture. Psalm 91:1-2 depict the essence of this chapter, "He who dwells in the shelter of the Most High will rest in the shadow of the Almighty. I will say of the Lord, 'He is my _____ and my _____ , my God in whom I _____ .'" This cripture is dealing with trusting God; Satan wants Jesus to believe it is about testing Him. Jesus, again, replies by reminding satan about the scripture in Deuteronomy 6:16, "Do not _____ the Lord your God as you did at Massah." Moses explains this improper testing of God in Exodus 17:7, "And he called the place Massah and Meribah because the Israelites _____ and because they _____ the Lord saying, 'Is the Lord among us or not?'" Jesus knows His scripture and will not be tricked into testing His Father.

Satan must have been terribly frustrated because his last attack was not as tricky as the first. In Matthew 4:8-9 he offers Jesus the, "kingdoms of the world and their splendor." All Jesus had to do was "bow down and worship" Satan. I believe this last attack wasn't as tricky because Satan spoke the truth. He does have dominion over this world ... for now. I John 5:19 states, "We know that we are children of God, and that the whole world is under the _____ of the _____ _____." But Jesus again returns to scripture and reminds Satan about Deuteronomy 6:13, "Fear the Lord your God, _____ him only and take your oaths in his name."

Jesus never changes His cleaning tactics. Satan tests and Jesus responds with scripture!

Ladies, we must continually clean the garbage out of our ears with God-dipped Q-tips. I suggest you carry these Q-tips with you everywhere; you never know when your ears will become dirty and a princess would be so embarrassed with green stuff sticking out of her ears!

The following are some ways I carry my Q-tips:

1. Reading the Bible every day and underlining key scriptures
2. An index card holder with scripture verses in my car console
3. Post-it note scriptures on my bathroom mirror
4. Scripture taped to my light switch
5. Framed scripture in my house and office
6. CD of the Bible in my car

Some new ideas I want to implement:

1. Bible verses on my iPhone (my newest Q-tip)
2. Podcasts from previous sermons on my iPod
3. Using more scripture in my lesson plans and research articles

Please add your personal ideas to this list:

_____

_____

Week 5 · Day 23

Eardrum music is another cleaning mechanism. A Q-tip cannot clean your eardrums. In fact, these cotton swab boxes usually have a warning that reads "CAUTION! DO NOT PLACE IN EAR CANAL." This warning is necessary because too many people have accidentally burst their eardrum while cleaning their ears. Ouch! God does not want His little girls hurting themselves in the ear cleaning process. He loves us so very much. So the inner ear, with the trickier to reach gunk, needs a different cleaning tool: praise music! The music reaches all the way to your eardrums and bounces off, thus creating a cleaning effect. Think of this process like cleaning a throw rug. You take the rug outside, hang it over a clothesline and then beat it with a broom. Every time you "beat" the rug, dust, dirt and grime falls off. The same scenario takes place in your inner ear.

Let's pretend you were just at the grocery store and the people in front of you were gossiping non-stop about some issues at your church or school. You try to divert your attention elsewhere; however, their words still make it into your ears. As you are leaving the store a car radio is blasting a vulgar song full of "colorful language." Dear sister, you are now walking through the parking lot with some green, nasty stuff in your ears. Whether you realize it or not, the gossip and "colorful language" is rattling around in your head. You load your groceries, start your car, and begin singing along to the local Christian radio station. Those songs begin to "beat" the tar out of your eardrum and break free the ugly residue placed there earlier.

Ugly words leave a big impression! Allow me to share a story to emphasize this truth. Ray and I were at a local restaurant with our sons. Raymond

Alan was about 4 at the time. We were enjoying watching them color and snacking on the peanuts when all of a sudden Raymond said a very bad word. The first time he said it Ray and I looked at each other like, "Naw, he didn't just say &^%$. But then he repeated it three or four more times, louder and louder with each effort. We were flabbergasted. Where did our innocent little boy hear this word? Then we heard it, too. A group of young men, at a close-by table, were using this word as a verb/pronoun/adjective/noun ... oh my. Ugly words leave a big impression! Praise music is your deep cleaning strategy. When you cannot remember scripture, God will bring a tune to mind.

Tomorrow you will spend some time exploring the notion of blood earrings.

Your Homework:

End today's time with God by writing out your ear cleaning regime.

When do you plan to listen to Christian radio? What CDs will you place in your car? Should you put a CD player or iPod in your office? Should you update your iPod and remove/replace songs to add some praise music? I suggest falling to your knees and asking God to open your eyes to ways you can protect and clean your ears. You learn the world around you through your ears. That is how you learned to speak and make meaning of your surroundings. Where will you place your God-dipped Q-tips?

Day 24: Wearing Blood Earrings?

"Take the other ram, and Aaron and his sons shall lay their hands on its head. Slaughter it, take some of its blood and put it on the lobes of the right ears of Aaron and his sons, on the thumbs of their right hands, and on the big toes of their right feet. Then sprinkle blood against the altar on all sides." (Exodus 29:19-20)

Please go back and re-read those verses, but this time underline everything the priest was supposed to do with the blood.

This chapter in Exodus is teaching us how Moses would induct men into the priesthood. Unlike the president of the United States' inaugural process, which is full of pomp and elaborate speeches and follow-up celebrations, the consecration of the priests was an incredibly solemn and multi-faceted process that occurred over a seven-day period. These steps involved: cleaning, clothing, anointing, sacrificing and blood daubing/sprinkling. Today's devotion deals with the blood daubing/sprinkling phase. The blood was placed on the right ear, thumb and toe to be a physical symbol that these priests are now part of a most sacred occupation and must present their ears, hands and feet as holy instruments to God. Their ears must be ready to hear the Word of God (we will discuss the hands and feet later).

This ritual was not created so the people could entertain God; it was not some kind of performance. This process was created to remind these men of their great role in the process of offering sacrifices for the sins of men. Ladies, we are in a similar but far greater position than these men. The priests were called to an occupation in the church—we are called into His family! Let me prove this point to you. Read the following verses and fill in the pertinent blanks:

John 15:14 "You are my _____ if you do what I command."

John 15:15 "I no longer call you _____, because a servant does not know his master's business. Instead, I have called you _____ , for everything that I learned from my Father I have made known to you."

John 18:36 "Jesus said, 'My kingdom is not of this world. If it were, my _____ would fight to prevent my arrest by the Jews. But now my kingdom is from another place.'"

Now read what Jesus says in John 20:17, after He had died on the cross and risen again!

"Jesus said, 'Do not hold on to me, for I have not yet returned to the Father. Go instead to my _____ and tell them, I am returning to my Father and your _____ , to my God and your God.'"

Yes, you read these verses right. Jesus, the Holy One, the One Without Sin, God's perfect Son, just called us His sisters and His Father our Father! That verse gives me the goosebumps. It also reminds me that with great privilege comes great responsibility!

I believe as princesses to the Great King we need daily physical reminders of our royal status. No, I do not think we should all place blood, or ketchup or food coloring on our right ear lobe. (But I must confess I thought about it.) But we must have some sort of ritual that will remind us of our daily obligation to be ready to hear God's Word and the voice of the Holy Spirit with us.

Phase 1—Most of us daily apply perfume or scented lotion. I am going to ask each of you to apply this scent in a new fashion by dabbing it on or behind your ears. As you go through this procedure pray and ask your Father to open your ears to hear His voice — either in the printed Word, the nudging of the Holy Spirit, or through His people. This process will only take a few seconds; however, it will serve as a daily reminder to prepare each day as a princess.

Phase 2—I believe our lives are similar to the ocean. Throughout each day the waves rise and fall. Some days and weeks we experience smooth water with very small waves. Then the storms of life come and we are found in the midst of serious trial. It is at these points that I believe we need additional reminders. Ladies, this time in our life should find us dressing like we are readying for battle. Not only should we pray while dabbing our daily scent behind or on our ears, we should wear our cross earrings. As of today I do not own a pair; but I can guarantee that I will soon. My wedding ring is a daily reminder that I promised, before man and God, to be faithful to my husband. I like that he wears his ring; it makes me smile to see that he also has that reminder to be faithful to me! I believe these earrings can serve that same purpose. They can remind us of His great sacrifice to us. Our Brother, the Holy One of God, died so we can be in His family. When we are suffering we need to remind ourselves that He still loves us and intimately knows our pain. He hurts with us.

The physical reminder of the earrings can also help us filter out the world's lies: God has abandoned you; How good is a God that allowed this to happen to you; why love a God that shows you His love in this fashion. They can also help us remember to focus on His love and promises for us.

If you do not have pierced ears, you can easily draw a cross on the back side of your earlobe. Right now this idea may seem ludicrous to you; however, when you are in the midst of a storm and the world around you feels wicked and unkind, this simple act can remind you, dear princess, of your royal status and the appropriate manner in which to respond.

Your Homework:

Please read Esther 2:12-16. How can her preparation be compared to our daily preparations as God's little girls?

_____
_____
_____
_____
_____

Week 5 · Day 24

Day 25: Wearing God-Ordained Princess Sunglasses?

Have you ever noticed that your outfit can affect your mood? What do you wear when you want to feel comfy? _____. How about when you want to feel pretty? _____ Or professional?

Your outfit also impacts the people around you. Ray's uncle is a farmer. He is an old-school, money management kind of guy. One night he went to the car dealer to purchase a new car. He went straight from work wearing faded blue jeans and a flannel shirt. The sales people did not appear in any hurry to help him. He finally had to ask for help; I believe the new girl was asked to help him. Lucky for her because Ray's uncle quickly found his brand new car and paid for it in full with cash! People do tend to judge one another based on outward appearances. That worldly habit is why we must begin wearing God-ordained princess sunglasses.

Read Galatians 2:6a and fill in the appropriate blanks. "As for those who seemed to be important—whatever they were makes no difference to me; God does not judge _____ ... ." God's ways are most certainly not the same as the world's methods!

God-ordained princess sunglasses must see beyond the outward appearance of the person.

Example #1—Elijah

World's view

2 Kings 1:8 "They replied, 'He was a man with a garment of _____ and with a _____ his waist.'"

1 Kings 17:5-6 "So he did what the Lord had told him. He went to the Kerith Ravine, east of the Jordan, and stayed there. The _____ brought him bread and meat in the morning and bread and meat in the evening, and he drank from the _____ ."

The world would have called him "bird man" and termed him a bit crazy. He dressed funny and spent way too much time alone!

God's view

2 Kings 2:11 "As they were walking along and taking together, suddenly a chariot of fire and horses of fire appeared and separated the two of them, and _____ went up to _____ in a whirlwind."

Matthew 17:2-3 "There he was transfigured before them. His face shone like the sun, and his clothes became as white as the light. Just then there appeared before them Moses and _____ , talking with _____ ."

God saw a man that cared more about pleasing Him than anyone else. In God's eyes Elijah was worthy of heading to heaven without passing through death!

Example #2—John the Baptist

World's view

Matthew 3:4 " _____ clothes were made of _____ , and he had a leather belt around his waist. His food was _____ and wild honey."

Week 5 · Day 25

The world would have called him "locust lover" and deemed him crazy. He also dressed funny and spent too much time alone!

God's view

John 1:32-33 "Then _____ gave this testimony: 'I saw the Spirit come down from heaven as a dove and remain on him. I would not have known him, except that the one who sent me to baptize with water _____, 'The man on whom you see the Spirit come down and remain is he who will baptize with the Holy Spirit.'"

John 1:6-7 "There came a man who was sent from _____; his name was _____. He came as a witness to testify concerning that light, so that _____ _____ all men might believe."

God saw a man that cared more about pleasing Him than anyone else. God spoke to John and gave him the heavenly task of paving the way for Jesus! I would love for God to speak in an audible manner with me!

Example #3—Saul

World's view

I Samuel 9:2 "He had a son named _____, an impressive _____ _____ without equal among the Israelites—a head _____ than any of the others."

I Samuel 10:24 "Samuel said to all the people, 'Do you see the man the Lord has chosen? There is no one _____ among all the people.' Then the people shouted, "_____ the king!'"

The world would have called him "eye candy" and made him a superstar. He was tall and handsome.

God's view

I Samuel 13:9 & 13 "So, he said, 'Bring me the burnt offering and the fellowship offerings.' And _____ up the burnt offering. 'You acted foolishly,' Samuel said. 'You have not _____ the _____ the Lord your God gave you; if you had, he would have established your kingdom over Israel for all time.'"

I Samuel 22:18 "The _____ then ordered Doeg, 'You turn and strike down the _____.' So Doeg the Edomite turned and struck them down. That day he killed eighty-five men who wore the ephod.

God saw a man that cared more about pleasing himself than anyone else. God took away Saul's kingdom. God sees our inner thoughts—no matter how pretty our outsides look!

God's view is often very different from the world's vision. Elijah and John the Baptist did not appear to be beautiful. I don't think any of us girls would have been fighting over who got to go to the dance with them. Seriously, hairy clothes and an animal hide belt was not the style of the day. The men we would have been attracted to would have worn fine linen clothes. Also, one was a "bird man" and the other a "locust man." Again, I don't see any of us women falling head-over-heels for either of them. Yet, God saw them as magnificent and lifted them to incredible status in His kingdom.

Saul, on the other hand, sounds like "eye candy." He was tall, handsome and ruler of a kingdom. Sounds like the making of a fairy tale. But God sees past the outward appearance and into the heart. The Israelites hurt God when they requested a king. God gave them a man that fit their need for a "physical ruler" (I Samuel 8:6-21); but this man clearly did not desire to serve the Lord with all his heart, mind and soul.

When we wear God's glasses we: 1) see past the physical attributes and outward actions to the hurting people behind them; 2) see a lost and scared world; and 3) see the real spiritual battle going on all around us.

Pick a pair of sunglasses and nominate them to be your new "God-ordained, princess sunglasses." Every time you wear them they should remind you to see people in God's eyes.

Your Homework:

I believe it is critical that you make this activity personal. I would like you to fill in the following table using real-life, personal examples. The following is my example:

1. Seeing past the action to the hurting person behind it

My eyes see: My sister trying to convince me to eat a handful of red "candy" until her friend stops me and yells, "That much speed could have killed her!" I see a sister who hates me.

God's eyes see: A lonely girl in serious pain who desperately wants her mom to stop looking at her sister and start loving on her.

2. Seeing a lost and scared world

My eyes see: Homosexual couples in almost every TV show I try to watch. It makes me want to write a mean and ugly letter to the TV producers.

God's eyes see: Hurting people turning to other hurting people because they have believed the lies Satan has told them.

3. Seeing the real spiritual battle going on all around us

My eyes see: A Christian school rampant with sexual sins and deception. This school has story after story of teachers and students committing sexual sin.

God's eyes see: Satan's minions hovering over this school and latching onto weak, unsuspecting individuals. (God's vision makes me want to pray over this school ... my vision makes me want to close this school.)

Your turn:

1. _____

2. _____

3. _____

Week 5 · Day 25

Week 6

Day 26: Always Pick Your Shoes Carefully -- Stiletto Heels?

Shoes can make a mediocre outfit sparkle and shine or destroy a perfectly matching set of clothing. For example, a pair of jeans with a pink button-down shirt is a "nice" outfit. Now add black boots lined with soft pink fur, the fur barely peeking out from the top, and you have an outfit that women will comment upon (Wow, I really like your outfit. Those boots are a perfect match for that shirt.) Now picture you wearing those same boots with white walking shorts and a soft pink polo shirt. Yes, you will get comments… probably not ones you will want to hear, though. White canvas shoes, with a bit of pink around the laces, would be a better match for that summer outfit.

Fellow princesses, our Father wants us to choose our steps carefully, which is why we must purposefully select our shoes. The shoes we wear can depict our intent. I wear my Nike shoes when I am on the elliptical trainer, attempting to burn off the calories I ingested while eating a carrot cake muffin. I select my hiking boots when I am going to walk the paths of the Blue Ridge Mountains. My fur-lined slippers accompany me throughout the house. A trip to the community pool calls for the use of flip-flops. The shoes usually express how I plan to spend my day.

Too often, though, Satan tricks us girls into wearing "shoes" that completely go against what our brains tell us we should do. Today's devotion will offer us a glimpse into the lives of women who were caught in sin due to inappropriate shoes (actions).

5" Stiletto Heels

Stiletto heels get their name from the stiletto dagger because both items have long, thin, pointy tips. These shoes can have heels that range from 1 to 8 inches in height. Try to picture the heels as long icicles. This metaphor is an important one because I believe the 'melting ice' heel allows us to fully understand how "slippery" these shoes can become.

The shoes were originally created to add height. I am 5'2" and married to a 6'3" man. I adore the idea of adding 5 inches to my height. However, the stiletto heel is more commonly associated with bringing women beauty due to their physical appeal. Men tend to like them because they offer the illusion of longer and slimmer legs, smaller feet, and cause the woman's calves, legs, and butt muscles to flex when walking.

Of course our calves, legs and butt muscles flex when wearing these shoes, our body is diligently working to keep us from falling or tripping! Personally, I find these shoes uncomfortable and painful. In fact, scientists have compared the pressure that is exerted on the tip of a stiletto heel to that of an elephant standing on one foot! That is a lot of pressure. So, our toes get jammed into the tip of our shoes, the bottom of our feet get forcefully pressed against the ground, our ankles strive to keep our feet properly attached to our legs, all while our body is desperately attempting to stay upright, which often requires us to press our shoulders back and jut our chest forward.

Our brain must concentrate on simply keeping us safe, which can lead us to walk without looking around, hence what I call the "stiletto scenario." I observed this strange phenomenon while in Hawaii. The whole family had decided to hike up a volcano. Parts of the hike included 60-degree climbs. These steep areas were a bit frightening. My whole family wore gym shoes or hiking boots. However, several Japanese girls wore 5-7" stiletto heels. I couldn't believe my eyes. Those girls wore the heels the entire hike. At first I was a bit envious. I thought, "Wow, I would like to look that cute while hiking." But the longer I watched them the more I felt the need to pray for them. They were so concerned with looking good that they never looked around on this beautiful hike. Every time I watched them their eyes were glued straight ahead as they concentrated on their next steps. They missed the beautiful setting completely.

Satan wants us to wear "stiletto heels" because it causes our brain to focus on something else, anything other than the good advice from God's Word. I believe the Bible provides several examples of women walking around in stiletto heels and then finding themselves in the areas they knew were forbidden by God.

Eve, the First Woman to Wear Stilettos?

God had one simple rule. He told Adam and Eve, "… but you must not eat from the tree of the knowledge of good and evil, for when you eat of it you will surely die" (Genesis 2:17). It appears that Adam and Eve fully understood the importance of this rule. Eve told Satan in Genesis 3:2, "We may eat fruit from the trees in the garden, but God did say, 'You must not eat fruit from the tree that is in the middle of the garden, and you must not _____ _____, or you will die.'" It seems that Adam and Eve decided they wouldn't even touch the fruit! You cannot eat fruit you don't touch, right? So Satan knows he has to get them to at least touch the fruit; thus, the stiletto heel scenario is necessary. Satan must distract Eve in order to get her thinking about anything but God's words.

I know that Eve was naked in the Garden of Eden, and she was not literally wearing shoes. However, I picture her wearing stiletto heels because her brain appears to be so busy talking to the serpent, and wandering about the garden, that she does not notice Satan leading her to the forbidden tree. Genesis 3:2 tells us that the tree was located _____ of the garden. I don't think Adam and Eve spent a great deal of time in this area because of how Eve responded in Genesis 3:6a: "When the woman _____ that the fruit of the tree was good for food and _____ to the eye … she took some and _____ it." It seems she was surprised by the fruit's pleasant appearance.

Satan knew that he needed Eve to see the beauty of the fruit to entice her to eat it. So, he lured Eve down a path to the forbidden tree and used the stiletto scenario by distracting her with questions and conversation. Satan did not drag her, kicking and screaming, to the middle of the garden. He didn't hold her head and make her gaze upon the beauty of the fruit. He did not pick the fruit and place it in her hands. He did not force her to open her mouth and ingest the fruit. All he did was distract her from thinking about God's words and lure her feet to a forbidden area.

Psalms 119:105 tells us, "_____ _____ is a lamp to my feet and a light for my path." We must focus our brains to concentrate on God's Word and ignore the many distractions (stiletto scenarios) of this life.

Lot's Daughters and Stiletto Heels in the Mountains?

By now I am praying that you realize that stiletto heels are anything that causes us to be distracted and forget the good counsel of God's word. Too often our feet take us places our minds know we should avoid!

I am confident Lot's daughters knew about God's laws and His grace, mercy, and love.

Fact #1—According to Genesis 12:4, who went with Abram on his God-inspired journey? _____

Genesis 12:7 & 8 depict Abram worshipping and communicating with God by building _____ . Even if Lot's daughters were not around for this part of his life (I am not convinced they were not, though), their father would have spoken about the uncle who loved him so much he gave him the best of everything (read Genesis 13:9-11).

Fact #2—Lot and his family were kidnapped by opposing kings (Genesis 14:12). Genesis 14:14-16 depicts Abram risking his life to save, "…his relative Lot and his possessions, together with the women and the other people" (16b). The girls watched their uncle save them from a life of captivity. Then they watched their uncle's God-inspired response to the king of Sodom's reward offer. Genesis 14:22-23 states, "But Abram said to the king of Sodom, 'I have raised my hand to the Lord, God Most High, Creator of heaven and earth, and have taken an oath that I will _____ _____, not even a thread or the thong of a sandal, so that you will never be able to say, 'I made Abram rich.'" Wouldn't you be impressed by a family member who risked his life to save you and then refused millions of dollars in reward simply because the king was not God fearing?

Fact #3—Angels saved Lot's daughters from being molested and destroyed by evil men. Genesis 19 depicts Lot bringing home two angels who were sent to destroy Sodom and Gomorrah. The sheer ugliness of that city is depicted in verses 4-5, "Before they had gone to bed, all the _____ from every part of the city of Sodom—both young and old—surrounded the house. They called to Lot, 'Where are the men who came to you tonight? Bring them out to us so that we can have _____ _____ them.'" Lot replies in verse 8a by saying, "Look, I have two daughters who have never slept with a man. Let me bring them out to you, and you can do what you like with them." Can you imagine the look on these girls' faces? But verse 11 shows the angels saving Lot and the girls by making them _____ so they could not find the door to the house. I don't know about you girls, but I would be praising a God who sent His angels to save me from these wicked men! But the story doesn't end there. In verse 16 the angels, "… grasped his hands and the hands of his wife and of his two daughters and _____ them _____ out of the city, for the Lord was merciful to them."

Week 6 · Day 26

I believe I have established that these girls were acutely aware of God, His rules, and His love. As a result, I am confident Lot's daughters were aware of the curse of Ham. Please read Genesis 9:18-27 and fill in the blanks.

1. Noah was _____ (v. 21).
2. Ham saw his father's _____ (v. 22).
3. Ham shared his sinful thoughts (the Bible does not tell us what they were) with his _____ _____ (v. 22).
4. Shem and Japheth do not join in the sinful thoughts and choose to honor their father by _____ (v. 23).
5. Noah tells Ham that his son Canaan will be _____ to Shem and Japheth (vs. 24-27).

Lot's daughters had to have heard about this dreaded curse. Their heads were full of the wisdom of God's words to avoid sin and the examples of their God-fearing uncle. Yet, the stiletto scenario allowed them to walk right into Satan's trap.

Your Homework:

Please read Genesis 19:30-38 (the story of how Israel's great enemies were born) and then answer the following questions.

In your opinion, what was the sisters' stiletto distraction? (Eve's was the serpent's questions and discussion.)

_____
_____
_____
_____
_____

Satan is not very creative. How is this sad story similar to Ham's?

These girls acted like they were imprisoned in their mountain living arrangements. What similar event in their past should have encouraged them to trust in God?

Do you have any stiletto scenarios in your life? What causes your mind to become distracted from turning to God's Word for the answer?

Day 27: Always Pick Your Shoes Carefully – Wearing In-line Skates?

Have you ever felt God asking you to do something that was a bit scary or unusual? Your heart tells you to make a move and your mind confirms this action with God's Word; however, your feet are determined to remain in their current location. It is almost as if Satan has superglued them to the ground.

My family recently heard our Father telling us to move to Virginia. Ray and I had well paying, successful careers and a large home in South Florida. I often started my day by floating in my heated swimming pool — in my pajamas. God and I would just float and talk. Ray was building amazing high rise structures in Miami, Fort Lauderdale, Key Biscayne, and West Palm Beach. He enjoyed his job and the people he worked with. Yet, God made it abundantly clear that we should trust Him and move. We now live in a teeny, tiny townhome in Virginia. Ray is building small projects with a group of people he barely knows. It is too COLD to swim even if my pool moved here with me (which it did not). Our income is significantly less. But, we obeyed God's call and are beginning to understand His plan for us. Although we miss the warm coastal breezes and the sound of palm trees, we want our Father to be happy with us.

Ray's "feet" remained in Florida for about six months. When he did move he looked like he was on in-line skates; he appeared a bit nervous and unsure of his footing. My husband never looks nervous or unsure. Once Ray realized that moving was part of God's plan for our family he moved fast and sure, though. It was like his body had become familiar with the in-line skates as he allowed them to move him quickly and efficiently to fulfill God's will.

Ladies, our Father often gives us in-line skates, places them on our feet, and laces them up nice and tight. He wants to help us move around quickly so we can follow His call in our life. But Satan sells us the lies, "Uh, oh, these skates are wobbly and ugly. You better stay right where you are or you are going to fall right on your face!" If we buy those lies we can become frozen with fear.

Today we are going to spend some time with women who were wearing God's in-line skates. God needed them to do something that was a bit scary. He knew they needed to move fast or the world and Satan's lies would prevent them from achieving His calling.

In-Line Skates

The daughters of Zelophehad wore in-line skates!

Numbers 26:33 tells us, "Zelophehad son of Hepher had no _____ ; he had only _____ , whose names were Mahlah, Noah, Hoglah, Milcah and Tirzah." American women may have a difficult time understanding the dire circumstances that faced these young ladies. Women in America vote, have important jobs, own homes, and are active in politics. The five daughters of Zelophehad lived during a time when women relied on men for everything. In fact, many Eastern cultures still see women in this light.

These five women lived during the time when Moses was dividing up the Promised Land amongst the tribes (Numbers 26:52-56). These young women most certainly heard all their relatives enthusiastically talking about the land they were about to inherit. I am guessing their relatives would begin whispering when one of the girls was nearby, knowing the girls were entitled to no inheritance. Their cousins were considered legitimate heirs to the land because their fathers had lineage proof of their affiliation with the, "… clan of Gilead son of Makir, the son of Manasseh, who were from the clans of the descendants of Joseph … ." (Numbers 36:1).

Can you imagine hearing all your neighbors, family members, and clan talking about the land they were about to inherit knowing that you were entitled to none of it? These poor girls had to be extremely frustrated and sad. Their father was dead. Now they had to rely on their uncles to assume their responsibility. I do not believe their extended family would have allowed them to starve or be without shelter. However, who is going to marry any of these women? None of them had anything to offer. They have no land inheritance and they have been living in a tent following Moses around in the desert. They didn't even have an established home. Even if they were extremely beautiful, the first man to marry any of the sisters would have been expected to assume responsibility for finding husbands for the rest of them. Since women were expected to bring a dowry, this financial and emotional burden would have scared away most men. These five young ladies were in serious trouble!

But God did not abandon them in their time of need. In fact, God was leading these young women to speak to Moses, to request their land, and to claim their rightful inheritance. Yet women were trained to remain quiet and allow the men to take care of the business items. I am confident all five of these women were terribly afraid. I picture them concluding their family meeting and slowly standing. Then I visualize them looking at their tent flap and feeling the discomfort of God's in-line skates. Their feet felt heavier than normal. The ground under them appeared shaky and unusual. Satan was whispering in their ears, "Don't go to Moses and Eleazar the priest. They will laugh at you. The whole assembly will scorn your attempts. You are weak and unworthy women. Your father died and now you must pay the price of his sins. He didn't have sons because he was a sinner. You are his curse. Now you must simply embrace this curse. There is nothing you can do about it. Save the little bit of dignity you have left and sit back down!"

Then the little one, Tirzah, began to move. Her feet actually glided along the surface. Her smile was infectious and she looked at her sisters and said, "Sisters, let us hurry, God has made our feet swift!" Then Numbers 27:1b-4 depicts all five girls doing the unthinkable, "They approached the Tent of Meeting and stood before Moses, Eleazar the _____ , the _____ and the whole _____ , and said, 'Our father died in the desert. He was not among Korah's followers, who banded together against the Lord, but he died for his _____ and left no sons. Why should our father's name disappear from his clan because he had no sons? Give us property among our father's relatives.'"

Can I get an "AMEN?" These girls followed God's calling and braved a scary audience. They even testified that their father's sin was his alone. Oh, ladies, we are excellent at claiming other people's sins. We hold can hold onto them when God is telling us to drop them and skate on over to His throne for healing and fellowship.

Now let's read what God said to Moses about these girls. Numbers 27:5-7 states, "So Moses brought their case before the Lord (smart man) and the Lord said to him, 'What Zelophehad's daughters are saying is right. You must certainly give them property as an inheritance among their father's relatives and turn their father's inheritance over to them.'"

I believe Moses brought their case to God because he had no idea what to do. I am sure his heart hurt for these young women; however, women did not own property. I can see Moses asking God, "Oh Lord, help me know what to do. The people are looking to me to answer these girls. They are already fighting about who gets the most land and who they have to share with. I want to help these girls but the people could revolt if I give them land. Oh God, tell me what I should do for I am lost here." I could be wrong, but can't you picture Moses talking to God in that fashion?

These five young women felt the warmth of God's embrace as they obeyed His voice and made their feet move forward when their body wanted to stay frozen with fear. In fact, Numbers 36:12 gives us the "Disney ending" with, "They _____ within the clans of the descendants of Manasseh son of Joseph … ." Yes! They all met and married wonderful men and lived happily ever after in the land God had given them.

Hannah Wore In-Line Skates!

Have you ever known someone who desperately wanted a child? Their thoughts become consumed by this desire. Going to the grocery store can become painful because pregnant women and moms with children are everywhere. I have been blessed with two sons; however, God did allow me a glimpse into the pain these women feel. I told you earlier that after five months of pregnancy I lost our first son. My body felt lonely. I began to hate my own body because it seemed to reject the life that I wanted so desperately. Then it seemed like pregnant women were everywhere. I remember telling Ray, "I think that pregnant women are following me. They seem to be everywhere I go." I was trying to make fun of a serious feeling while also crying for help.

The day the doctor removed the "remainder" of my first pregnancy he also scheduled a three-month follow-up appointment. During this visit the doctor asked me questions and checked my physical symptoms. A few minutes into the exam he stopped and told me to "go pee in this cup." I found his request a bit odd, but complied. I soon learned that God had allowed me to become pregnant again. Nine months later I gave birth to a 10-pound, 21-and-a-half inch healthy baby boy, Raymond Alan Jones III. I only had to yearn for a child for three months, but it felt like a lifetime of waiting. I cannot fathom how poor Hannah felt.

Hannah loved her husband, Elkanah. But she had to share him with another wife, Peninnah. That part alone would be horrible. But I Samuel 1:4-7 shows us the pain Hannah had to endure. "Whenever the day came for Elkanah to sacrifice, he would give portions of the meat to his wife _____ and all her sons _____ daughters. But to Hannah he gave a double portion because he _____ her, and the Lord had _____ her _____. And because the Lord had closed her womb, her _____ kept provoking her in order to irritate her. This went on _____ after _____. Whenever Hannah went up to the house of the Lord, her rival provoked her till she _____ and would not _____."

I had to wait three long, painful, sad months for another pregnancy. I cannot imagine waiting years and years while being purposefully tormented about my failure to get pregnant! My heart hurts for poor Hannah.

I picture Hannah pushing her food around on her plate; her stomach in too much pain to eat. Then the thought occurs to her to ask God to give her a child. "I am right here by the house of the Lord," Hannah might have thought, "I could even offer to give my child back to Him ... if only he would allow me to conceive and give birth to a child." I am guessing that Hannah thought about this idea before. Today, however, she acted upon it by using her in-line skates to race her to the house of the Lord before she talked herself out of it, again.

I Samuel 1:10-11 depicts Hannah's actions: "In bitterness of soul Hannah _____ much and _____ to the Lord. And she made a _____, saying, 'Oh Lord Almighty, if you will only look upon your servant's misery and _____ me, and not forget your servant but give her a _____, then I will give him to the _____ for all the days of his life, and no razor will ever be used on his head.'"

Her feet followed God's desire for her to ask Him for help, and God answered in a big way. I Samuel 1:20 states, "So in the course of time Hannah conceived and gave birth to a _____. She named him _____, saying, 'Because I asked the _____ for him.'" Hannah was given a child!

But Hannah would need quick feet again soon. Now she must return her son to the house of Lord. I would find that part so difficult. In I Samuel 1:22 Hannah tells her husband, "...After the boy is weaned, I will take him and present him before the Lord, and he will live there _____." Ladies, I am going to be completely honest here, if I were Hannah, my son might have never been officially "weaned." Taking him to Eli, knowing he would never return home, would be extremely difficult. But Hannah laces up her in-line skates and immediately follows the actions God desires. She brought Samuel to Eli when he was only about 3 years old!

God rewarded Hannah's faithful actions. I Samuel 2:21 tells us, "And the Lord was _____ to Hannah; she conceived and gave birth to _____ sons and _____ daughters ... ." I Samuel 2:19 also shows us that Hannah never lost an opportunity to let Samuel know she loved him. It states, "Each _____ his mother made him a little _____ and took it to him when she went up with her husband to offer the annual sacrifice." Hannah loved her little boy; she also loved the God who gave Him to her enough to obey His will.

Your Homework:

Read I Samuel 25:1-40.

Why was David offended by Nabal's rude treatment (14-16)?

_____
_____

How is Abigail described (3)? _____
_____
_____

How is Nabal described (3)? _____
_____
_____

Circle the verse in which Abigail "laces up her in-line skates."

Verse 14 or Verse 18

Reread verses 28-31. Why are these words so wise? _____
_____
_____

_____

_____

_____

Who killed Nabal (37-38)? _____

How is Abigail rewarded (40)? _____

_____

_____

Sometimes our Father wants us to "rip off the Band-Aid" and quickly follow His calling. If we wait we risk becoming afraid and allowing self-doubt to block our feet.

Week 6 · Day 27

Day 28: Always Pick Your Shoes Carefully – Wearing Spiritual Slippers!

There is something about slippers that makes people feel at home and comfortable. I have a pair of pink slippers under my desk at work. Every now and then I forget to take them off when I make the mad dash to the ladies room. The responses on the college students' faces always let me know I have my slippers on, though. Their eyes smile and they say things like, "Oh, I like your slippers" or "Wow, those look comfy" or "Aren't you the cute professor." Big football players respond with the same soft look when they see me moving around the halls in my business suit and slippers.

I wear the slippers because my feet get cold and they help me feel at home when working in the office. I also used slippers to positively affect the environment when I taught elementary school. My students could bring in their slippers and wear them in the classroom. At the end of the day their chairs were placed on their desks with their slippers set on top of them. Each morning they would put their book bags in their cubby, switch their shoes for slippers, and sit down to begin writing in their journal while soft music and indirect lighting set the tone. I wanted my students to feel the warmth of home in our classroom!

Ladies, we need to regularly put on our spiritual slippers. These slippers should be soft, incredibly comfortable, and inviting. They should entice others to approach us and inquire about our relaxed and peaceful stance. In other words, these shoes allow us to share the gospel with a lost and dying world! Isaiah 52:7 reinforces the need for God's daughters to wear spiritual slippers. It states, "How beautiful on the mountains are the _____ of those who bring _____ , who proclaim _____ , who bring good tidings, who proclaim _____ , who say to Zion, 'Your God reigns!'"

More importantly, ladies, is the fact that Jesus tells us to wear these shoes. In fact, He states this need when He is praying to God on our behalf. He had just talked to God about His disciples when he began to pray for future believers, which we now know is us. John 17:20-23 states, "My prayer is not for them alone. I pray also for those who will _____ in me through their message, that all of them may be _____, Father, just as you are in me and I am in you. May they also be in us that the world may _____ that you have sent me. I have given them the glory that you gave me, that they may be one as we are one: I in them and you in me. May they be brought to complete unity to let the _____ know that you sent me and have _____ them even as you have loved me." See what I mean? I told you so! Jesus wants us to wear our spiritual slippers and softly entice the world into knowing the love of God and the salvation Jesus brings.

Spiritual Slippers

Angelina the adulterer put on spiritual slippers

Angelina was born with thick dark hair and big blue eyes. The midwives and local women all talked about her beauty and whispered about which man was really her father. Abandoned at an early age by her mother, Angelina was raised by her grandmother. However, she always wondered about her mother and father and why the other kids whispered things about her.

Then the impossible happened. Her mother returned to town and took Angelina home with her. Angelina was aglow with the hope of love and family. Her hopes were soon dashed by the realization that her mother had married a man and started a new family with him; her role was to help with the kids and stay out of their way. Angelina decided to be as good and helpful as she could be, then her mother and father would surely love her. Years of silent obedience passed and yet her parents ignored her efforts, severely chastised her errors, and lavishly poured their affections on her half brother and sister. Her whole body longed for love and attention.

As Angelina grew up she quickly realized that young men smiled at her and paid her attention. Her hunger for love naturally drew her to these men. Sadly enough, it wasn't long before Angelina was seeking love in all the wrong ways. Now her worst nightmare was unfolding before her eyes. The whole town was looking at her and disgusted. No one loved her. No one ever did or ever would. She couldn't believe the religious Pharisees, the same ones who liked to look at her, were dragging her out into the middle of the town. Her heart raced and her entire body began to shake and sweat as these religious leaders shoved her in front of Jesus.

"Teacher, this woman was caught in the act of adultery. In the Law Moses commanded us to stone such women. Now what do you say (John 8:4-5)?"

Angelina quickly looked up to see the eyes of yet another man she thought would disappoint her. She couldn't believe what she saw, though. As her eyes met Jesus' eyes she became overwhelmed by His great love and sadness for her. She felt as if He experienced every tear she ever cried, each moment she searched for love and was left alone, every day she had lived and felt unloved and unworthy. For the first time in her entire life, Angelina felt true love and compassion!

"This poor man," Angelina thought.

"They are going to use my sins to hurt him. If He has the crowd stone me, they will no longer listen to His message. If He stops them, they will say He doesn't follow the law."

"I have ruined yet another person's life," she thought.

"But Jesus bent down and started to write on the ground with his finger. When they kept on questioning him, he straightened up and said to them, 'If any one of you is without sin, let him be the first one to throw a stone at her (John 8:6b-7).'"

Angelina froze with fear. Surely many of the religious men around her would immediately begin hurling the stones. She began to calculate how many people around her were without sin. Her body began to hurt from the protective stance. Every muscle was straining to provide security and safety. Time passed and slowly she looked up to see she was alone with Jesus.

"Where did they all go?" she thought. "What is Jesus writing?"

Then those loving and understanding eyes met hers again.

"Jesus straightened up and asked her, 'Women, where are they? Has no one condemned you?' 'No one, sir,' she said. 'Then neither do I condemn you,' Jesus declared. 'Go now and leave your life of sin (John 8:10-11).'"

As you ascertained I added some narrative details to this very real Bible account. However, I truly picture this scene in that fashion. I believe this woman left Jesus feeling loved and realizing that everyone makes mistakes and sins. She had a choice to turn her life around. I see Angelina putting on her new slippers and telling everyone who asks her, "Where are your sexy old shoes?" about Jesus and His great love!

We are no different than Angelina. Each of us has a story, an amazing, life-changing and true story about what Jesus did for us. That is the story we must share with the world. Our slippers should lead our feet to lost people and allow us to enter into conversations about the weather, the day, the war, our shoes … and then about God's great love for them!

Your Homework:

Picture yourself wearing your slippers. You have just come home from work, shopping, school, working out … you take off your shoes and slip on your slippers. You turn on the radio and it begins playing Mercy Me's "I Can Only Imagine." You sit down in your favorite chair and cuddle up with your favorite throw blanket.

Describe your body language:

Shoulders _____

Hands _____

Facial expression _____

Mouth _____

Now picture yourself standing in a busy shopping mall (around Christmas). People are frantically moving about and bumping into one another. You are standing in a long line waiting to buy some merchandise. Can you put on your spiritual slippers? Can you picture yourself at home, on your chair, with your slippers ... all safe and comfortable? If you can, the people around you will want to know why you have peace in the midst of chaos. They will be drawn to your calm demeanor.

What are some ways you can begin a conversation with people?
_____
_____
_____

How can you casually plant a seed about the great love of Jesus without making people defensive? _____
_____
_____
_____

I might say something like, "Oh, wasn't that person nice when he held the door for her. I bet that action made Jesus smile," or "Can you believe this great sale today? It looks like you found some great deals. Isn't God so good to us!"

What could you say?

Day 29: Beautiful Busy Hands

The hands of a princess are beautiful. They are delicate and soft like the petals of the fairest rose. Her nails are polished and immaculately shaped. These hands are adorned with gold and fine gems, the jewelry depicting her regal and pampered status.

Okay, girls, now we can wake up from our daydreaming. Yes, a princess' hands are beautiful, but their beauty is not, according to the world's standards. Today we are going to spend some time learning how God sees beautiful hands.

The Proverbial Woman has Beautiful Hands!

Proverbs 31:10-31 describes a woman of noble character. Many of these verses can assist us in understanding what her hands may have looked like. Please read the entire section and then complete the following verses.

31:13 She selects wool and flax and works with _____ hands.

31:14 She is like the merchant ships, bringing her _____ from _____ .

31:15 She gets up while it is still _____; she provides _____ for her family and portions for her servant girls.

31:16 She considers a field and buys it; out of her earnings she _____ a vineyard.

31:17 She sets bout her work _____; her arms are _____ for her tasks.

31:19 In her hand she holds the distaff and _____ the spindle with her _____ .

31:20 She opens her arms to the poor and extends her _____ to the needy.

31:22 She makes coverings for her _____ ....

31:24 She _____ linen garments and sells them, and supplies the merchants with sashes.

31:31 Give her the reward she has _____, and let her _____ bring her praise at the city gate.

Do these verses give you the impression that a daughter of God has soft and well manicured hands? I am not saying it is wrong for us to work at having pampered-looking hands. I am stating that it requires effort because God has called us to have working hands. Our hands are meant to be busy preparing, purchasing, polishing, purifying, producing and providing many comforts for the people we love and those who are less fortunate than us. As a result our hands can become weather-beaten, waterlogged, and weary. But, ladies, God sees them as more beautiful than diamonds because they show signs of doing His work!

Working Ruth had Beautiful Hands!

Ruth is a princess. Her name is literally found in the genealogy of Jesus! Matthew 1:5 states, "Salmon the father of Boaz, whose mother was Rahab, Boaz the father of Obed, whose mother was _____." What an amazing honor!

Ruth was one special woman. So how did she use her hands?

Her story begins in Ruth 1:1, "In the days when the judges ruled, there was a famine in the land, and a man from _____ in Judah, together with his wife and two _____ went to live for a while in the country

Week 6 · Day 29

of Moab." The famine brought Ruth's first husband to her land. This family consisted of Elimelech and Naomi and their sons Mahlon and Kilion. Shortly after arriving in Moab, tragedy strikes and _____ dies (1:3). However, the boys met and married Moabite women, Ruth and Orpah, and lived with Naomi for 10 years. Then Ruth 1:5 tells us, "both Mahlon and Kilion also _____ , and Naomi was left without her two sons and her husband."

Naomi needs a change in scenery; I can fully understand why. So, all three women leave Moab to return to the land of Judah. Think about that last sentence. Both daughter-in-laws were willing to follow Naomi to her hometown. Naomi must have been a loving and kind woman. Naomi convinces Orpah to return to her mother and search for a husband; however, Ruth refuses to leave Naomi.

Here is where we learn about Ruth's hands. Naomi and Ruth had to travel from Moab to Bethlehem. A long and arduous journey with men, yet these women only had each other. I believe both women's hands were work worn and weary.

When these women arrive in Bethlehem, "the whole town was stirred because of them, and the women exclaimed, 'Can this be Naomi?'" (Ruth 1:20). I believe these women were overwhelmed by her change in appearance; her face and body must have shown her rough journey and the pain of her circumstances. In fact, Naomi tells these women (vs. 20), "Call me Mara, because the Almighty has made my life very bitter." This sad scene is the environment in which Ruth is "welcomed" into her new community. This scenario has all the necessary components for the perfect pity party. Oh how I can get lost in a good pity party! My friends all gathered around, feeling sorry for me, while I sit down and bask in my sad circumstances. I recount my troubles, they tell me how bad they feel for me, and I recount my troubles some more. If I am not careful I can have permanent "pity party friends," girlfriends who feed my need to recount my troubles and just talk about how unfair life is to all of us.

Your Homework:

Your job today is to uncover how Ruth used her princess hands to prevent a pity party and bring prosperity and honor to Naomi.

Read Ruth 2:2-7.

How did Ruth use her princess hands to help Naomi? _____
_____

Fill in the blanks to verse 7: "She said, 'Please let me glean and gather among the sheaves behind the harvesters.' She went into the field and has worked _____ from morning till _____, except for a short _____ in the shelter."

Please picture Ruth going through the process of picking up leftover grain and describe the process here:

_____
_____
_____
_____
_____
_____
_____

Her body must have hurt! My hands, back, neck and legs would be crying out for rest. The time in the sun would deplete all of my energy. Ruth 1:16-17 shows Ruth using her words to demonstrate her love for Naomi. But Ruth 2:7 depicts Ruth using her hands to demonstrate her love for Naomi and God.

Week 6 · Day 29

Ray will often respond to our boys' claims with the following statement, "That is what your mouth says!" It is his way of challenging our boys to put their words into action.

My question for you today is: Are your words and deeds synchronized? Write out all the things to tell God, your friends, and family you want to accomplish. Then write what actions you are implementing to accomplish these goals. Finally, write the word "steadily," "sometimes" or "rarely" next to the action. I have included two examples.

Statement	Action	Description
To keep a cleaner home	Laundry Dusting Vacuuming	Steadily Rarely Sometimes
To love God more	Pray without ceasing Read God's word Respond in love to unkind people	Sometimes Steadily Rarely

Now write out your action plan!

Day 30: Beautiful Uplifted Hands

Yesterday we spent time learning about the "dishpan hands" of a daughter of the King, hands that literally get dirty in the process of serving and loving God and His people, hands that are engaged in the business of completing the daily task of our royal status. Today we are going to explore hands that praise God, the other key ingredient to having true princess hands. The following vignette portrays the need for balance.

The soft sounds of even breathing brought a smile to his face. Watching his teenage daughter sleep reminded him of their earlier days. Closing his eyes he remembered it vividly. He would walk in the room, sit on her bed, and gently rub her back. Even before she opened her eyes he would whisper, "Guess who loves his little girl?" Lillian always responded with the same soft giggle and retort, "You do, Daddy. But I love you more!" Then they would try to outdo each other with "why I love you" reasons. His favorite response was when she would say, "I love you because you take such good care of me Daddy."

The sound of his daughter's alarm clock brought him back to the present. He watched her arm quickly hit the snooze button as she tried to go back to sleep.

"Lilly, darling, it is time to start your day."

No reply.

Gingerly sitting on her bed he began to gently rub her back.

"Dad, really, I can get 15 more minutes of sleep. Please, just go to work, I can take care of myself now," she grunted.

"Okay, honey, I just ... wanted you to know I love you."

His little girl responded by rolling over and waving him off with her hand.

"Bye, Lilly. I put your lunch money on the kitchen counter. Please make sure you put the new car insurance card in the glove box of your car.

"Yeah, okay, Dad ... BYE already!"

Through barely open eyes Lilly watched her dad leave the room. "What is his problem?" she thought to herself. "He seems so unhappy lately. He should be thrilled that he has a daughter who gets straight A's in school and hasn't wrecked her car. I get myself off to school every day and even make dinner for him a couple of nights a week. What more does he want from me?!"

Then, as if reading her mind, her father turned in the hallway to get one more glimpse of his little girl. The look of loneliness permeated his features.

"Hey Dad," she whispered. "Thank you for the lunch money. I love you, too."

To Lilly's amazement her father's face lit up like the sun breaching the horizon.

Didn't her dad realize that she loved him? Then she tried to think about the last time she had told him those words. She had been so busy trying to be the good daughter that she forgot to take the time to tell him how much she cared. Her father daily sacrificed to make her life comfortable. How could she forget to thank him?

"Oh Lilly, girl, I love you! Have a great day, honey," her father replied.

As she watched her smiling dad walk away she realized she was happy. It was early in the morning and she was happy? Early mornings usually meant grumpy feelings. Yet, making her dad's whole face smile left her feeling good and weirdly refreshed.

"Wow," she whispered to herself. "Making my dad happy still makes me happy. I am such a nerd."

But in the quiet of her room Lillian asked God to help her remember to thank her dad and tell him she loves him more often.

Too often we can become the teenage daughter. We take all of the things God does for us for granted and assume He knows we love and appreciate Him because of our deeds. But our Father, the Lord God Almighty, wants a relationship with us. The Bible shows us His desires to use our hands to nurture a relationship by: 1) talking to Him, 2) lavishing Him with our love, and 3) praising Him.

Example #1—Using Your Hands to Talk to God

Genesis 3:8-9 "Then the man and his wife heard the sound of the Lord God as he was walking in the garden in the cool of the day, and they hid from the Lord God among the trees of the garden. But the Lord God called to the man, 'Where are you?'"

Before sin entered the world, God spent time with people by physically _____ with them.

I truly enjoy going on walks with my husband. The temporary absence of the television and household needs allows us to simply visit and catch up on each other's day and dreams. Recently I noticed that when Ray and I are engaged in a conversation we will use our hands to convey meaning. Some examples are that I often grab his arm if I want him to understand the importance of my topic; or we usually hold hands while discussing our dreams; or our hands become animated when we are trying to get each other to understand our point of view.

Can you imagine God, in His physical presence, walking with you? Can you see the intimate relationship He desires? Now try to picture yourself

walking with God and becoming so engrossed in the conversation that your hands join the conversation! Too often we approach God out of habit; we bow our heads, say "thank you for the food" or "please give us safety," and then get on with our routine.

Example #2—Using Your Hands to Lavish Him with Your Love

There is a significant difference between using our hands to fulfill our royal duties and using them to purposefully lavish our love upon Him. Some of my duties as a mom are to make school lunches, wash dirty clothes, and grocery shop. These acts allow me to take care of my family and indirectly demonstrate my love for my boys. But my relationship with my boys would be superficial if I did not physically demonstrate my love for them. A hug after a football game, holding their hands when we pray, scratching their backs, a morning hug, an encouraging pat on the back, and a gentle touch to the face are all some ways I use my hands to lavish my boys with love and affection.

So how do you physically lavish God with love? We know we cannot touch Him because Moses was only allowed to see the back of God (Exodus 33:19-23). But our hands must "touch" Him to bring us into a close relationship with Him.

So how do we touch God? _____

_____

_____

To "touch" God we must: _____

_____

_____

Confess Before Men that Jesus is Lord and Savior.

Matthew 10:32: "Whoever _____ me before men, I will also acknowledge him before my _____ in heaven."

How would you feel if your best friend pretended she didn't know you when you were in public? What if you only had a private relationship? Our love for Jesus should permeate our face, actions and reactions.

Acknowledge that Jesus is the Bridge that Spans Us to God.

Hebrews 4:14: "Therefore, since we have a great _____ _____ who has gone through the heavens, Jesus the Son of God, let us hold firmly to the faith we profess."

Hebrews 7:25: "Therefore He is able to save completely those who come to God _____ Him, because He always lives to _____ for them."

You need Jesus to talk to God. Without Him you are lost in a dying world. Do not forget this truth; it will make you have a thankful heart!

Lavish Our Love Upon His Son!

Mark 1:11: "And a voice came from heaven: 'You are my _____, whom I love; with you I am well _____ .'"

Make sure you thank Jesus, daily, for His great love and sacrifice for you. Pour your love upon Him like the woman pouring expensive perfume on His feet (Mark 14:3). The perfume was incredibly costly so the people rebuked her (Mark 14:4). Your time is more precious than money. Ray often says, "I can always make more money but I cannot make more time." Give Jesus one of your most precious commodities and lavish Him with your time. Tell Him how much you love Him. Reserve time for just Him and you.

Example #3—Using Your Hands to Praise and Exalt Him

Singing in church is like clapping your hands at a football game except you are offering your praise to the Most High God! Do not let anyone interfere with your efforts to praise God. I get easily distracted by cute babies or adorable outfits so I have to sit in the first few rows at church (much to Ray's dismay). I also have to ask Jesus to clear my mind and help me to focus on praising Him for all He does for me. Then my voice lifts with fellow believers and I literally feel the presence of God. I will never forget the first time this worship experience happened. When I opened my eyes I was surprised to see my uplifted arms. Then I realized I lifted them so I could feel closer to touching my Heavenly Father; I actually responded to His presence without worrying about what people around me would think. I felt 20 years younger and completely in love with God. I did not want to leave the sanctuary that day. My poor husband had to sit patiently while I said my "goodbyes" to this mind-blowing experience. The presence of God just rattled my world.

I wish I could say every worship encounter leaves me feeling as if I have literally touched my Heavenly Father, but I cannot. I can, however, state that I work diligently to uncover what is holding me back from this encounter. Am I withholding forgiveness? Am I thinking about other things instead of concentrating on God's great love? Think of it this way: you want every worship encounter to be like a winning touchdown during the Super Bowl … you are thoroughly excited and overwhelmed by all the touchdowns in your life and cannot stop applauding God for His greatness!

Your Final Homework: The Royalty Oath

Please take your time to thoroughly read and complete the following document. Your weekly lessons will help you with this process. I recommend printing it and placing it on a mirror or another location that will daily remind you of your royal status and ensuing obligations.

I, _____, am a daughter of the Most High God. My royal status is established through accepting Jesus as my Savior. As a princess I realize I must:

Week 1

Embrace my l_____ story and use it to share how My Father has changed my life.

Trust God and be an _____ of love.

Week 2

Be a reflective p_____, always striving to improve my relationship with God.

Be a prayer w_____, strategically improving my prayer life day by day.

Week 3

Prepare for s_____ and be ready to f_____ at all times.

Week 4

Guard my _____ .

Wash my mouth with f _____ ,
so _____ , c _____ , s _____ ,
and b _____ .

Week 5

Brighten my complexion through w _____ .

Apply lipstick that reminds me to en _____ ,
show em _____ , and share s _____ with
those around me.

Wear e _____ and s _____ that
remind me to be careful of what I see and hear.

Week 6

Avoid stiletto _____ distractions.

Embrace moments for i _____ _____ .

Remember to wear my s _____ , even while shopping
and working.

Week 6

Use my hands to eagerly s _____ others.

Actively use my hands while t _____ to God.

Week 6 · Day 30

Use my hands to "touch" God by I _____ Him with my love.

Use my hands to p _____ Him.

I AM precious.

I AM privileged.

I AM priceless.

There is NOTHING my Father cannot do.

I will work hard to make Him smile every day!

References

Graham, B. (2004). *The Classic Writings of Billy Graham: Angels, How to be Born Again, The Holy Spirit.* Edison, NJ: Inspirational Press

Kaya, N. and Epps, H. (2004). *Relationship Between Color and Emotion: a study of college students.* College Student Journal. Retrieved January 24, 2009 http://findarticles.com/p/articles/mi_m0FCR/is_3_38/ai_n6249223

Breinigsville, PA USA
30 November 2010
250345BV00001B/29/P